AMERICAN
GLASS BELLS

A. A. Trinidad, Jr.

AMERICAN
GLASS BELLS

A. A. Trinidad, Jr.

4880 Lower Valley Road · Atglen, Pennsylvania 19310

Library of Congress Control Number: 2009941081

Designed by RoS
Type set in Futura Lt/ Zurich Lt BT

ISBN: 978-0-7643-3417-7

Printed in China

Schiffer Books are available at special discounts for bulk purchases for sales promotions or premiums. Special editions, including personalized covers, corporate imprints, and excerpts can be created in large quantities for special needs. For more information contact the publisher:

Published by Schiffer Publishing Ltd.
4880 Lower Valley Road
Atglen, PA 19310
Phone: (610) 593-1777; Fax: (610) 593-2002
E-mail: Info@schifferbooks.com

For the largest selection of fine reference books on this and related subjects, please visit our web site at
www.schifferbooks.com
We are always looking for people to write books on new and related subjects. If you have an idea for a book please contact us at the above address.

This book may be purchased from the publisher.
Include $5.00 for shipping.
Please try your bookstore first.
You may write for a free catalog.

In Europe, Schiffer books are distributed by
Bushwood Books
6 Marksbury Ave.
Kew Gardens
Surrey TW9 4JF England
Phone: 44 (0) 20 8392 8585; Fax: 44 (0) 20 8392 9876
E-mail: info@bushwoodbooks.co.uk
Website: www.bushwoodbooks.co.uk

Dedication

**To my many bell collector friends at the American Bell Association
who have encouraged me to prepare this book on glass bells.**

Acknowledgements

The contribution of information from many bell collectors and
organizations has made this book possible. My thanks especially to
Marilyn Grismere, Mary and Ken Moyer, Kelsey Murphy, Sally and Rob
Roy, Jo Ann Thompkins, and Gail Bardhan of the Rakow Research Library
at the Corning Museum of Glass, for providing much information.

Contents

Chapter Four

Lampwork Bells

The American Bell Association   158

Index   159

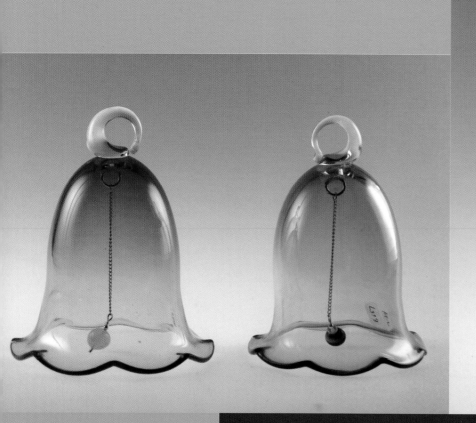

Introduction

Bells have been used as a means of communication and ornamentation in world cultures for over three thousand years. Generally, bells have been made of metal, porcelain, wood, clay, and glass. Among collectors you will find all types of bells. This book focuses attention on glass bells, presenting them by country of origin, type of glass, and manufacturer when known. When the manufacturer is unknown, the bells are presented as unknown or in a special grouping.

The prices for bells vary based on condition, age, number made, availability, and attractiveness to the collector. Therefore, for bells shown herein, a range of values generally has been shown.

In recent years, many bell producing companies have closed or merged with other companies. The attributions presented in this book are the latest the author has been able to determine. Bells previously shown in the author's books, *Glass Bells* and *Collectible Glass Bells of the World,* are not repeated in this book unless additional information has become available.

The author has gathered photographs from museums and bell collectors for this book. They are shown under the respective countries or producers to which they are attributed. The names of museums and collectors who furnished information are shown when requested or approved.

Chapter One

American Art Glass Bells

Lapsys Crystal Studio
Wheeling, Illinois
1976-

Raimundas Lapsys and Raminta Lapsys have been producing a variety of art glass items, including an occasional bell, using cold working and hot working glass techniques for over 30 years.

A Lapsys clear glass bell engraved with three birds, a nest, and tree branch. The handle is frosted glass, flat, and tapered. The label states that it was designed by R. Lapsys. 2.9"dia. x 5.25"h. $40-50.

Maslach Art Glass
Greenbrae, California
1971-

Steven Maslach made art glass bells that are popular with bell collectors. Most have an iridescent finish and are usually signed with a date along the inside rim.

A Maslach iridescent gold over blue glass bell with a three knop handle separated from the rest of the handle by a gold iridescent ring. Signed along the inside rim "Maslach 8-79". 3"dia. x 5.6"h. $100-150.

A Maslach iridescent silver over blue glass bell with a three knop handle separated from the rest of the handle by the third silver iridescent knop. No signature or date. 3"dia. x 5.8"h. $100-150.

A Maslach blue iridescent glass bell with a two knop handle separated from the rest of the handle by a blue iridescent ring.. Signed along the inside rim "From Crandon 1980". 3"dia. x 5.8"h. $100-150.

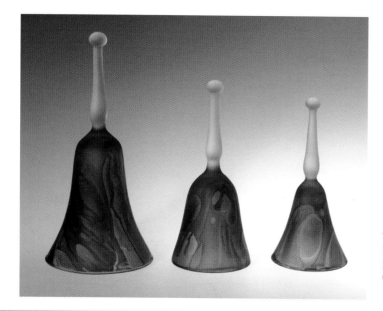

Nouveau Art Glass, Inc.
Roseto, Pennsylvania, 1970-

This company is known for its satin glass bells. The bells are hand painted and then chemically treated to give them a soft satin finish. The company also operates under the name Reuven Art Glass

Three Nouveau Art Glass Company bells of Reuven blue and violet satin glass in a flowing pattern. Left to right; 3.75"dia. x 7.6"h, 2.75"dia. x 6.1"h, 2.75"dia. x 5.5"h. $30-50.

Pilgrim Legacy Cameo Glass
Huntington Museum of Art
Huntington, West Virginia, 2002-

In March 2002, the Pilgrim Glass Company closed, but many blanks remained that had been used for making cameo glass articles. The Huntington Museum of Art made arrangements to have Pilgrim Glass artists, Dwayne Wallace and others, create new Pilgrim Legacy Cameo pieces. They used the remaining blanks, furnished by Pilgrim Glass owner Alfred Knobler, to make cameo pieces available in the museum shop. Among the cameo pieces made are several designs for glass bells.

A PLC cranberry/bone/clear cameo glass bell with elephants. "Follow the Leader", D32010, 1 of 5 produced 7/27/03. 3.9"dia. x 7.5"h. $300-350.

A PLC blue/bone/crystal cameo glass bell with flowers. "Morning Glory", D32016, 1 of 5 produced 10/6/03. 3.9"dia. x 7.6"h. $300-350.

A PLC ducks on black/bone/crystal cameo glass bell. "Mallard Morning", D32008, 1 of 5 produced 7/27/04. 3.6"dia. x 7.6"h. $300-350.

A PLC blue/bone/crystal cameo glass bell. "Town Crier", D32025, 1 of 5 produced 7/26/04. 4"dia. x 7.5"h. $325-400.

A PLC cranberry/bone/crystal cameo glass bell. "Cardinal Sings", D32011, 1 of 5 produced 7/19/04. 3.75"dia. x 7.5"h. $300-375.

Steuben Glass Works
Corning, New York, 1903-1933

Steuben Glass, Inc.
Corning, New York, 1933-

Between 1936 and 1962 Steuben produced several bells. The bell shown here is a smaller variation of a 6" similar bell produced in 1949. Earlier bells by Carder are also known.

A Steuben clear glass bell with an air twist handle. This bell is usually found in a 6" high version. 1.1"dia. x 4"h. $175-225.

Studios of Heaven
East Lynn, West Virginia, 2001-

After the Pilgrim Glass Corporation closed in 2001, Kelsey Murphy and Robert Bomkamp formed the Studios of Heaven to continue producing carved cameo glass items. Amongst them are bells.

Some cameo bells were made in five colors and crystal. The blank bells were made by Ron Hinkle with a hand pulled decorative handle after casing five colors and crystal. Then Kelsey Murphy and Robert Bomkamp carved through the colors allowing the images to appear in the correct color. The powder casing is very fragile so control is very important.

Burmese glass made by Fenton was used by Ron Hinkle to make blown glass bells with hand pulled decorative handles which were then cut by Kelsey Murphy and Robert Bomkamp to make the Jungle Bell series.

The first two bells shown are from the author's collection. The remainder has been provided through the courtesy of Kelsey Murphy. The larger bells are generally 3.5"dia. x 6.5"h. The smaller Jungle series bells are generally 3"dia. x 4"h.

A cased dark green on Burmese glass bell, "Fern Fantasy" with a pink closed wing bird handle. One of a kind bell made on June 3, 2008. #700816. 4.1"dia. x 7.9"h. $250-300.

A blue/crystal/green hot cased glass bell. "Spring Perch". One of a kind bell made in June 2005. #700433. 4"dia. x 5.8"h. $400-450.

Right:
A cased lavender on
Burmese glass bell,
"Dogwood Delight".
One of a kind made on
June 3, 2008. #700815.
$220-250.

Below, left:
A cased red on
Burmese glass bell,
"Deeply Clowning".
One of a kind bell
made on June 3, 2008.
#700818. $200-220.

Below, right:
A cased green on
Burmese glass bell,
"Fern Fantasy". One
of a kind bell with
open wing bird handle
made on June 3, 2008.
#700816. $220-250.

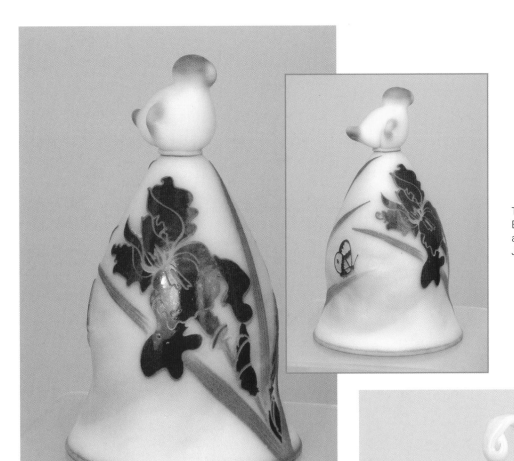

Two views of a cased lavender on Burmese glass "Burmese Iris". One of a kind bell with bird handle made on June 3, 2008. #700827. $200-220.

Two views of a cased purple on Burmese glass "Swan Pond". One of a kind bell made June 16, 2008. #700821. $250-275.

Two views of a cased black on Burmese glass "Panda Bell". One of a kind bell made September 6, 2008. #700849. $250-275.

Chapter One

Three views of a cased purple on Burmese glass "Little Birdie in the Tree". One of a kind made November 20, 2008. #700866. $250-275.

Three views of a 5 colors and crystal cameo bell in green, topaz, white, black, cobalt, and crystal. "Jungle Bell I". One of a kind bell made June 10, 2007. #700679. $400-450.

Chapter One

Two views of a 5 colors and crystal cameo bell. "Jungle Bell II". Made June 10, 2007. #700680. $400-450.

Two views of a 5 colors and crystal cameo bell. "Jungle Bell III". Made June 10, 2007. # 700681. #400-450.

Two views of a 5 colors and crystal cameo bell. "Jungle Bell IV". Made June 10, 2007. #700682. $400-450.

Chapter One

Two views of a 5 colors and crystal cameo bell. "Jungle Bell V". Made June 10, 2007. #700683. $400-450.

Two views of a 5 colors and crystal cameo bell. "Jungle Bell VI". Made June 10, 2007. #700684. $400-450.

Three views of a 5 colors and crystal cameo bell. "Jungle Bell VII". Made June 10, 2007. #700685. $400-450.

Zellique Art Glass

Benicia, California, 1980-2006

Over a twenty-five year period master glassblower and owner Joseph Morel created many vases, bowls, perfume bottles, paperweights, and a very few bells. The bell pictured is the only one seen by the author.

A multi-striped sector pattern in blue and gold glass with a three loop top of handle and top shaped glass clapper. Signed "J. McKeevy, Zellique 1990". 4.4"dia. x 8"h. $300-400.

Zimmerman Art Glass Company

Corydon, Indiana, 1944-

The Zimmerman Art Glass Company is a family operated business that manufactures primarily handcrafted glass novelties. Amongst them are finely crafted bells that were made by Barton Joseph Zimmerman, recently deceased co-owner and operator of the company.

A clear glass Zimmerman bell with a shoulder and handle of blue petals. 3.5"dia. x 5"h. Clear blue round glass clapper with etched "Z" and a metal star attachment on a chain to the bell. $70-100.

Two clear glass Zimmerman bells: the one on the left has a shoulder and handle of cranberry petals. 3.5"dia. x 6.6"h. The one on the right has a shoulder and handle of pale blue petals. 3.25"dia. x 5"h. Both have clear round glass clappers with etched "Z" and attached by a metal star on a chain to the bell. $70-100.

A clear glass Zimmerman bell with a shoulder and handle of green petals. 3.75"dia. x7"h. Signed "BZ07". $50-60. *Courtesy of Mary & Ken Moyer.*

A clear glass Zimmerman bell with a shoulder and handle of dark blue petals. 6.5"dia. x 2.75"h. Signed "Z07" $50-60. *Courtesy of Mary & Ken Moyer.*

A clear glass Zimmerman bell with a shoulder and handle of yellow petals. 3"dia. x 6.25"h. signed "Z08". $50-60. *Courtesy of Mary & Ken Moyer.*

A multicolored glass Zimmerman bell on a clear glass base. 3.25"dia. x 6.5"h. $55-70. *Courtesy of Mary and Ken Moyer.*

A multicolored glass Zimmerman bell on a clear scalloped glass base. 3"dia. x 5.5"h. $75-90. *Courtesy of Mary and Ken Moyer.*

Unknown

Two bells, believed by the author to be American, are shown as examples of nicely crafted glass bells.

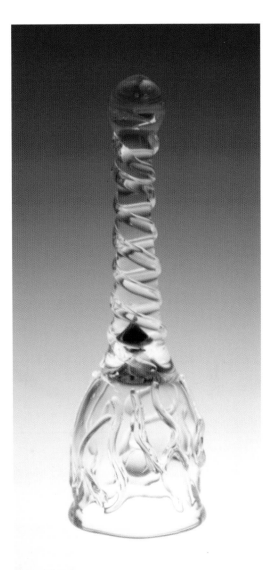

A clear glass bell with glass ropes around the bell and spiral handle with a marble top. 2"dia. x 6.5"h. $40-60.

A mottled gold, silver, and purple glass bell in four molded sections and a round clear wavy handle. 3"dia. x 4.5"h. $200-250.

Chapter Two
American Cut Glass Bells

Boston & Sandwich Glass Company
Sandwich, Massachusetts, 1870-1887

During its brief history the Boston and Sandwich Glass Company produced a few cut glass bells.

A blue cut to clear strawberry diamond and punties pattern glass bell with a clear glass hexagonal flat top handle. 3.1"dia. x 5.6"h. $700-900.

A cranberry cut to clear glass bell with punties, cross-cut diamonds, and ovals and a clear glass hexagonal handle with cut corners. 3.35"dia. x 5.75"h. $700-900.

A Russian pattern cut glass bell with a hexagonal flat top handle. 3.25"dia. x 5.75"h. $350-425.

A. L. Blackmer Company
New Bedford, Massachusetts, 1894-1916

Very few Blackmer cut glass bells are known. The one shown is also known in a larger size.

A Blackmer clear cut glass bell with an "Aetna" pattern and flat radial star pattern top of handle, c.1894. 3"dia. x 5.75"h. $375-425.

A Clark cut glass bell in a cross-cut diamond and strawberry diamond pattern, known as the Henry VIII pattern, with a bronze pineapple handle. 3.4"dia. x 5.5"h. $400-500.

T. B. Clark & Company
Honesdale, Pennsylvania, 1884-1927

The Clark Company produced bells distinguished by the crosscut diamond and star top of handle. The A-E bell shown with a 12 pt. star in the middle of the hobstar is also known with an 8 point star.

A Clark cut glass bell in the A-E pattern with a typical handle cut with a 12 point radial star pattern on top and cross-cut diamond on the side at the top. 3"dia. x 5.5"h. c.1901. $500-700.

C. Dorflinger & Sons
White Mills, Pennsylvania, 1865-1964

Dorflinger cut glass bells are known with four different cut designs for the top of handle. Based on known existing bells and a Dorflinger Salesman Book there are at least twenty different pattern Dorflinger cut glass bells known to exist. These are American, Belmont, Brilliant, Colonial, Dresden, Hob Diamond, Lorraine, Marlboro, Oriental, Parisian, Renaissance, Roxana, Royal, Russian, Savoy, Star & Diamond, Strawberry Diamond & Fan, Sultana, No. 28, No. 40, and at least two unidentified patterns which may have been made as a special order. Known Dorflinger cut glass bell sizes are 5 ½", 5 ¾", 6", 6 ¼", 7 ¼", 7 ½", 8", and 8 ½" high.

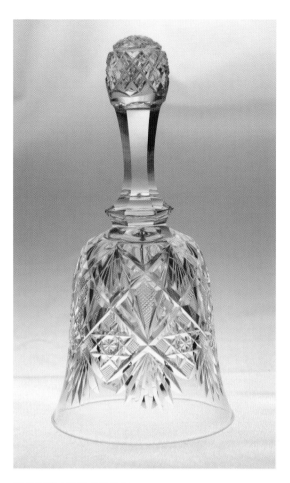

A Dorflinger cut glass bell in the Marlboro pattern. 3.6"dia. x 7.5"h. $900-1,100.

A Dorflinger cut glass bell in a green cut to clear glass #28 pattern. 3"dia. x 5.75"h. $2,500-2,800.

A Dorflinger cut glass bell in the Brilliant pattern. 3.6"dia. x 7.24"h. $1,200-1,400.

A cut glass bell, possibly Dorflinger, cut with a 3 horizontal cut variation of the Renaissance pattern. 3"dia. x 4.25"h. $375-425.

A cut glass bell, possibly a Dorflinger bell, with a 3 horizontal cut variation of the Renaissance pattern, inscribed with "World's Fair 'script L' 1893". The bell may have been made for Libbey for the inscription to be done at the Libbey pavilion at the fair. 3"dia. x 4.5"h. $700-750.

A Dorflinger cut glass bell in the Savoy pattern. 3"dia. x 5.4"h. $600-800.

While Dorflinger is well known for its cut glass bells, during its later years some blown glass bells were produced.

A Dorflinger blown clear glass bell with mottled colored specks and round handle. 4"dia. x 7"h. $300-350.

T. G. Hawkes & Company
Corning, New York, 1880-1962

The Hawkes company produced a variety of bells during its long history. During all its years Hawkes recycled broken stemware by replacing the base of the stem with a round tapered sterling silver handle, furnished by the Gorham Manufacturing Company, and using a hollow metal clapper on a chain attached to the glass in a drilled hole. It is not known how many of these bells in a particular pattern were made. Some may be one of a kind. All their bells used the drilled hole and plaster in contrast with most other cut glass companies that used a twisted iron wire embedded in the glass to hold the chain or wire that held the clapper.

Bells earlier than 1915 used a special heavy silver sinker shaped clapper. Because of bells being broken by these clappers, Hawkes used some wood clappers for a short time, and then replaced them with a lighter sinker type clapper for a few bells. After 1915, a two-part hollow metal ball clapper, used by most other cut glass companies, was used for their bells.

The company, well known for its cut glass bells, also produced some bells in clear undecorated glass. In later years, Hawkes produced a variety of bells supported on sterling silver stands.

A Hawkes clear glass bell with a hexagonal flat top handle. Signed HAWKES on the shoulder. 2.75"dia. x 4.5"h. $100-125.

A Hawkes cut glass bell in pattern #182 with a sterling silver handle. 2.75"dia. x 5.5"h. $100-125.

A Hawkes cut glass bell in the Puritan pattern with a sterling silver handle. 2.6"dia. x 5.75"h. $100-125.

A Hawkes glass bell cut and engraved with a floral pattern with a sterling silver handle. 3.4"dia. x 7"h. $300-350.

A cut glass bell attributed to Hawkes. Beautifully cut floral pattern along the edges separating the large hexagonal oval cuts on the glass. Alternating large and small circular cuts along the edges of the hexagonal handle. 3"dia. x 6"h. $300-350.

A Hawkes thin glass inverted bowl, engraved with a floral pattern, sitting on a sterling silver post on a rectangular cut glass base, and supporting a metal striker. 5"h. $550-600.

A Hawkes inverted bowl with cut vertical lines and pointed ovals suspended by a sterling silver arm on a clear glass base with a sterling silver rod clapper. Signed HAWKES on the silver connected to the base. 3.5"dia. bowl and 6.5"h. $300-350.

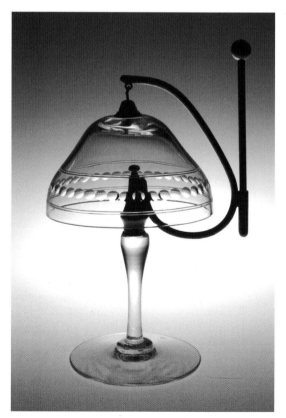

A Hawkes inverted bowl with a row of cut spots between two parallel cut double lines suspended by a sterling silver arm on a clear base and holding a sterling silver rod clapper. The base of the silver stem support is marked HAWKES STERLING S1274. 3.5"dia. x 6.5"h. $350-400.

J. Hoare & Company
Corning, New York, 1853-1920

Hoare bells can be identified by the distinctive cut of their handles; usually a tapered hexagonal cross-section with three horizontal miter cuts around the widest part. Known patterns are Crosby, Delft, Eleanor, Monarch, Pluto, and Tokio.

A Hoare cut glass bell in a Monarch pattern with the variation of an 8 point star inside the hobstar. 3"dia. x 4.6"h. $450-550.

A Hoare cut glass bell in a Delft pattern. 3"dia. x 4.5"h. $300-400.

A Hoare cut glass bell in the Eleanor pattern. 3"dia. x 4.6"h. $300-400.

A Hoare cut glass bell in strawberry diamond and fan pattern with a hexagonal handle and a multi-faceted top. 2.9"dia. x 5.5"h. $250-350.

Libbey Glass Company
Toledo, Ohio, 1880-1935

Several Libbey Glass Company cut glass bells are known as well as blown and decorated glass bells that were available in their pavilion at the 1893 Columbian Exposition in Chicago.

A Libbey cut glass bell in the Venetia pattern. 3"dia. x 4.5"h. $350-450.

A Libbey cut glass bell in Lily of the Valley pattern with a hexagonal handle with serrated corners. 3"dia. x 5.75"h. $350-450.

Maple City Glass Company
Honesdale, Pennsylvania, 1898-1927

Maple City produced many fine cut glass bells including some in the Flower Period from about 1916-1920s.

A Maple City cut glass bell in the Kent pattern. 2.6"dia. x 5.5"h. $150-200.

A Maple City cut glass bell in the Rosamond pattern. The base of the handle has an etched maple leaf mark. 3"dia. x 5.5"h. $300-400.

A Maple City cut glass bell in the Modena pattern. 3"dia. x 5.75"h. $200-250.

A Maple City cut glass bell in the Rosamond pattern. 2.9"dia. x 5.75"h. $300-350.

Meriden Cut Glass Company

Meriden, Connecticut, 1895-1923

Meriden is known for some bells produced in the Flower Period.

A Meriden cut glass bell in the Mayflower pattern. 3"dia. x 5.5"h. $250-300.

C. F. Monroe Company

Meriden, Connecticut, 1882-1916

The Monroe company is known for Wave Crest ware and metal objects as well as cut glass objects. A silvery metal and cut glass twister bell is illustrated in a Monroe Cut Glass catalog from the early 1900s as a No. 15 Y. W. Bell. The bell shown below is a similar bell except that the cut glass pattern is similar to the hobstar, cross-cut diamond, and fan pattern shown on the top of a No. 14 G. I. Jewel box shown in the same catalog.

A plan view of a Monroe cut glass and metal twister bell. 4"dia. x 4"h. $2000+.

A side view of the twister bell showing the four leg silvery metal base housing the bell.

Mount Washington Glass Company

New Bedford, Massachusetts, 1869-1900

Very few Mount Washington Glass Company cut glass bells are known and few have been found illustrated in publications.

A Mount Washington cut glass bell in the Wheeler pattern. 3.5"dia. x 7.1"h. $700-750.

Pepi Herrmann Crystal
Gilford, New Hampshire, 1974-

Pepi Herrmann has produced the finest cut glass bells since the Brilliant Period of American cut glass. Many have been produced in colored cut to clear glass in one-of-a-kind patterns.

A Pepi Herrmann Crystal emerald cut glass bell as their 2007 annual bell. 3.4"dia. x 7.5"h. $200-275.

A Pepi Herrmann Crystal amethyst cut glass bell in a vintage pattern. 3.4"dia. x 7.5"h. $300-350.

A Pepi
Herrmann
Crystal peridot
cut glass
bell in the
Romance
pattern.
3.4"dia. x
7.5"h. $250-
350.

Chapter Two

A Pepi Herrmann Crystal ruby cut glass bell in a vintage pattern. 3.4"dia. x 7.25"h. $300-350.

A Pepi Herrmann Crystal gold amber cut and engraved glass bell in the Anna-Linnea pattern. 3.25"dia. x 7.5"h. $300-350.

A Pepi Herrmann Crystal peridot cut and engraved glass bell in the Anna-Linnea pattern. 3.25"dia. x 7.5"h. $300-350.

Pitkin & Brooks Company
Chicago, Illinois, 1872-1920

Very few Pitkin & Brooks cut glass bells are known.

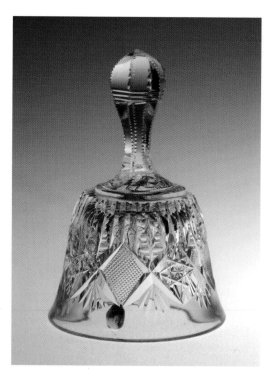

A Pitkin & Brooks cut glass bell in a Prism pattern. 3"dia. x 4.5"h. $225-275.

A clear cut glass bell attributed to Straus by a collector. 3.25" dia. x 6.4"h. $300-400. See a discussion of the design of similar bells on pages 46 and 47.

L. Straus & Sons
New York, New York, 1888-1925

Many fine bells in various patterns were produced by Straus. Some of their cut glass articles were produced in a factory above the Macy Department Store in New York City. Known patterns include American Beauty, Antoinette, Capri, Corinthian, Napoleon, as well as some patterns in the Flower Period. Most Straus bells have a distinctive multifaceted top of handle.

A Clear glass blank with a silver clapper used by Unger Brothers for their cut glass bells. 2.9"dia. x 4.75"h. $60-100.

Unger Brothers
Newark, New Jersey, 1901-1918

Unger Brothers produced bells in very few patterns. They usually have a solid silver clapper and chain.

Unknown

The author has seen many American cut glass bells which presently have not been identified. The later bells have the chain, holding a crystal clapper, inserted in a preformed hole filled with a plaster.

A small clear glass blank for a cut glass bell used for the following two bells of an unknown producer. 3"dia. x 4.6"h. $40-60.

A clear cut glass bell with a thumbprint pattern, 3"dia. x 4.5"h. $200-250.

A clear cut glass bell with crosscut diamond pattern in a bank of 4x4 and 2x2, and crossed bars pattern. 3"dia. x 4.5"h. $200-250.

Two American cut glass bells with patterns using a similar blank.. The bell on the left has a diamond pattern. 3"dia. x 6.1"h. The bell on the right has a floral cutting with a band of punties. 2.9"dia. x 5.9"h. Both have a hexagonal pointed handle and similar glass clapper. $100-125 each.

A rectangular bell with a cut diamond pattern on slanted sides and square handle. 2.1" x 2.6" x 5.4"h. $75-100.

Far right:
A cut glass bell with stars, crosscut diamonds and fans and a hexagonal cut handle with crosscuts on the edges. 3"dia. x 5.75"h. $200-250.

Right:
A cut glass bell with a flower and cherry pattern with a hexagonal cut handle. 3"dia. x 5.5"h. $200-225.

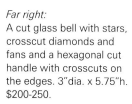

A cut glass bell with a buzz star pattern alternating with two stars and cross-cut diamonds. 3"dia. x 5.75"h. $150-200.

A clear cut glass bell with vertical cuts and punties pattern. 3"dia. x 5"h. $150-200.

A glass bell cut with vertical flutes and tapered hexagonal flat top handle. 2.75"dia. x 5.1"h. $70-85.

A clear cut glass bell with crosscut diamond pattern in a bank of 3x3 and 2x2, and a crossed bars pattern. 3"dia. x 4.5"h. $200-250.

The photos of four similar cut glass bells and two Dorflinger cut glass bells present a mystery in identification. All six bells have identical cut patterns on adjacent sides of the body of the bells, but research and discussions with knowledgeable cut glass collectors has not revealed the companies who made them. One book shows a bell similar to the four bells as being made by Libbey in a Corinthian pattern, but the consensus is that Libbey did not make them. A check with Dorflinger cut glass experts does not identify the pattern on the Dorflinger bells. The use of a crystal clapper, instead of the usual two part hollow metal clapper, indicates that they were probably made late in the Brilliant period. One of the four bells has a clapper missing. One of the two Dorflinger bells has a crystal clapper. The other has a replaced clapper. The author believes all six bells were made by the same company or perhaps by a person who cut glass for Dorflinger.

Two Dorflinger cut glass bells with cut patterns on adjacent sides identical to the four bells shown. The handle is cut in the Dorflinger strawberry diamond pattern typical of many Dorflinger bells. The chain holding a crystal clapper is attached to an iron wire embedded in the glass. Heights are 8" and 7.4". $800-1000.

Chapter Two

Four identical American cut glass bells cut with hobstar, crosscut diamond, and fans on one side and a crosscut diamond and fans on an adjacent side. Heights range from 6.5" to 5.5". All handles have similar cuts. Clappers on three bells are crystal and attached by chain to an embedded iron loop at the inside top of the bell. One bell has a clapper missing. A collector has attributed one of the four bells to L. Straus & Sons, but the author has not been able to confirm this attribution. $300-600.

A view on an adjacent side of the bells.

Chapter Three

American Blown & Pressed Glass Bells

This chapter also includes blown glass bells that have been engraved or etched.

Akro Agate Company
Clarksburg, West Virginia, 1911-1951

Akro Agate bells from the 1930s are known primarily in clear colorless glass as well as many colors in a smocking pattern. They sometimes used the clear colorless bells as covers for an assortment of perfume bottles embedded on a cardboard base.

Near the prongs holding the clapper the Akro mark of a molded flying crow holding two marbles can be found together with "Made in USA".

When Akro Agate closed in 1952, the bell molds were sold to the Guernsey Glass Company in Cambridge, Ohio. When the Guernsey company closed recently, the bell molds were sold to the Wilkerson Glass Company, Moundsville, West Virginia.

A clear Akro Agate smocking pattern bell used as a cover for a container holding three perfume bottles on a cardboard base. The base has a label for "Wheatley, 5th Ave., NY". 3.25"dia. x 5.6"h. $80-100.

A blue Akro Agate smocking pattern bell with a green swirl. 3.25"dia. x 5.6"h. $75-80.

American Cut Crystal Corporation

Hewlett, New York, 1934-

The company has had some glass bells made for them in Germany and Czechoslovakia.

An American Cut Crystal Corp. glass bell with cut vertical flukes made in Czechoslovakia for the company. 2.5"dia. x 5h. $25-40.

An American Cut Crystal Corp. glass bell with a frosted floral handle made in France for the company. 2.5"dia. x 6.75"h. $30-40.

Art of Fire

Laytonsville, Maryland, 1981-

Art of Fire was started as a contemporary glass studio in 1981. The studio produces hand-blown art glass mugs, champagne flutes, ornaments, and other glass items including bells.

Two blown glass Art of Fire bells in cranberry glass and blue glass with ruffled rims and loop handles. Signed "R. Foster" with a date of 7/87 for the pink bell and 5/87 for the blue bell. 4"dia. x 5"h. for the cranberry bell and 3.6"dia. x 4.75"h. for the blue bell. $35-50 each.

Avon Products, Inc.
Springdale, Ohio, 1939-

Avon has produced many types of glass bells, some of which are in the shape of a bottle with perfume. Many of their bells are strictly ornamental.

Clear glass bells, painted with flowers and colored crystal clappers for each of the 12 months, were made in France for Avon in 1986.

An Avon clear glass bell decorated with a butterfly and flowers. c.1998. 2.75"dia. x 6.75"h. $15-25.

Ten of twelve clear crystal Avon bells with applied colored floral decoration and colored crystal clappers for the months of the year. 3.1"dia. x 5.75"h. $20-30 each.

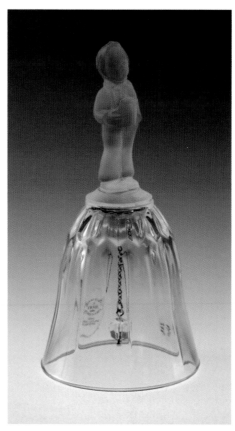

An Avon frosted "Soloist" on a clear molded glass base made by Goebel for Avon. c.1994. 2.75"dia. x 5.75"h. $15-25.

An Avon clear glass bell with frosted bird and flowers. 3.25"dia. x 5.75"h. $15-25.

An Avon clear glass bell with a flower and fruit ceramic handle and strawberry clapper. c.1989. 2.6"dia. x 5.4"h. $25-30.

An Avon clear glass bell with applied floral decoration and a molded floral handle. c.1992. 2.75"dia. x 6.5"h. $20-30.

Bacalles Glass Engravers
Corning, New York, 1966-1995

Some early bells in flashed ruby glass were made from blanks produced in West Virginia. Some clear glass bells have been engraved on blanks made in Europe.

A Bacalles clear glass bell with an etched butterfly and flowers. 3"dia. x 5.75"h. $30-40.

A Bacalles clear ruby blown glass bell with clear colorless handle. 2.6"dia. x 4.75"h. $20-30.

Blenko Glass Company, Inc.
Milton, West Virginia, 1922-

The Blenko Glass Company started as the Eureka Glass Company which specialized in mouth blown and colored flat glass. The company has produced a great variety of glass objects but few bells. Known bells have been produced to celebrate a special event.

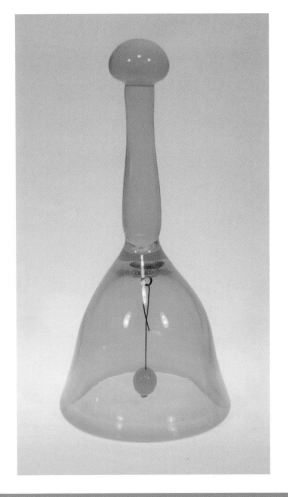

A unique Blenko clear yellow glass bell made in 1984 by Les Womack, master finisher, for his daughter's wedding. 3"dia. x 6"h. $200+

Boston & Sandwich Glass Company
Sandwich, Massachusetts, 1870-1887

The Boston & Sandwich Glass company produced several blown glass bells during their short time of operation. The bells generally show a painted decoration on acid etched glass.

Below:
A Boston & Sandwich clear glass bell with painted forget-me-knots. It has an imbedded twisted wire holding a chain with a two piece metal clapper. 3"dia. x 5.25"h. $150-175.

A Boston & Sandwich clear glass bell with painted floral decoration. 3"dia. x 5.5"h. $150-200,

A Boston and Sandwich clear ruby glass bell with a colorless handle. It has a twisted iron wire holding a replaced chain and clapper. 3"dia. x 5.5"h. $100-150.

A Boston & Sandwich frosted opal glass bell with an applied wreath of blue flowers. 2.75"dia. x 4.6"h. $250-300.

A Boston & Sandwich frosted opal glass bell with painted floral decoration. 3"dia. x 5.5h. $250-300.

A Boston & Sandwich cased yellow over white glass bell with painted flowers. It has an imbedded twisted wire holding a chain with a two piece metal clapper. 2.75"dia. x 4.75"h. $200-250.

Boyd's Crystal Art Glass Company
Cambridge, Ohio, 1978-

Boyd's Crystal Art Company has made bells from molds acquired from other glass companies. The company trademark is a B in a diamond sometimes found on the top of the bell handle.

Boyd's Crystal Art Glass bells in orange, chocolate, and vaseline glass. There is a 'B' in a diamond at the top of each bell. c.1980. 2"dia. x 3.75"h. $25-35 each.

The Bradford Editions
1973-

The Bradford Editions is one of the affiliated companies of The Bradford Exchange producing many collectible items. In 1996 they produced some glass bells as part of a series called Heaven's Little Helpers.

A 1996 Bradford Exchange clear glass bell with a ceramic handle of a praying angel sitting on a cloud with the moon behind. The clapper consists of a group of golden stars. The bell is labeled "Praying For Beautiful Days" and is the fourth issue in the Heaven's Little Helpers bell collection series. 3"dia. x 5.5"h. $30-40.

A Brooke Glass frosted glass bell with painted yellow flowers for October; one of a series of bells of the month. The handle is metallic. 2.5"dia. x 5.4"h. $25-35.

Brooke Glass Company, Inc.
Wellsburg, West Virginia, 1983-2001

Brooke Glass produced glassware for the lighting industry as well as glass novelties, including a few bells.

Bryce Brothers Company
Mt. Pleasant, Pennsylvania, 1895-1965

Bryce Brothers is known to have made bells with a top shaped handle in the 1940's. The Lotus glass Company bought the bell molds from Bryce Brothers and produced some similar handle bells. Based on a company 1916 catalog, Bryce Brothers also made bells with a twisted round and hexagonal base handle.

A Bryce Brothers blue glass bell with a clear colorless top shaped handle. 3.1"dia. x 5.4"h. $75-90.

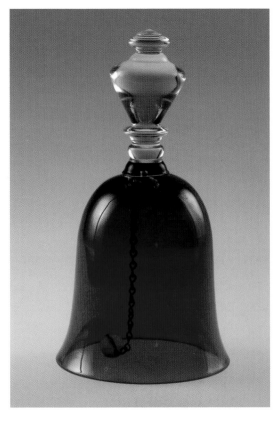

A Bryce Brothers ruby glass bell with a clear colorless glass top shaped handle. 2.75"dia. x 5.1"h. $75-90.

Cambridge Glass Company
Cambridge, Ohio, 1902-1958

Cambridge produced many high quality items including some bells from 1932 into the early 1950s.

A Cambridge Glass Company clear glass bell, shape #3121. 3"dia. x 5.5"h. $30-40.

Central Glass Company
Wheeling, West Virginia, 1867-1939

In the early part of the twentieth century Central produced bells typically with a twisted tapered handle on a hexagonal base similar to those produced by Bryce Brothers.

The hollow metal two-part clappers are on a chain which is held by a twisted iron wire embedded in the glass.

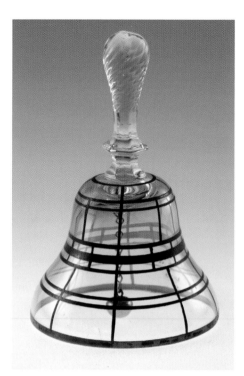

A Central Glass Co. clear glass bell with silver bands and a round twisted handle on a hexagonal base. Two-part hollow metal clapper. 3.25"dia. x 5"h. $125-150.

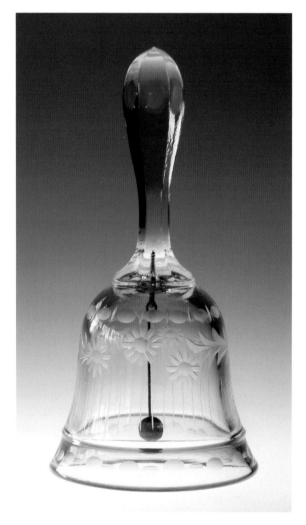

A Central Glass Co. clear glass bell with engraved daisies and punties and raised rim. 3.25"dia. x 6.25"h. $75-100.

A Central Glass Co. clear glass bell with a cut floral pattern and raised rim. The hexagonal tapered handle is cut along the edges. 3.25"dia. x 6.25"h. $75-100.

A Central Glass Co. clear glass bell with a twisted dark blue handle. Two-part hollow metal clapper. 3.25"dia. x 5"h. $75-100.

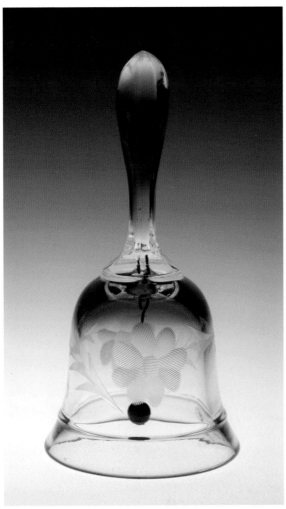

A Central Glass Co. clear glass bell with a cut floral pattern and raised rim. 3.25"dia. x 6.25"h. $75-90.

A Central Glass Co. clear glass bell with a cut floral pattern on the main part of the bell and the raised rim. 3.1"dia. x 6.26"h. $65-90.

Beaver Falls Co-operative Flint Glass Company
Beaver Falls, Pennsylvania, 1879-1889

Co-operative Flint Glass Company, Ltd.
Beaver Falls, Pennsylvania, 1889-1937

The Beaver Falls Co-operative Flint Glass Company was started in February 1879 in Beaver Falls, Pennsylvania by a group of glass workers who left the McKee factory in Pittsburgh. The name was changed in 1889 to the Co-operative Flint Glass Company, Limited.

Starting in 1886, several publications reported that the company had produced a butter dish with the bell as a cover. Based on this information all the butter dishes and bells, made in a three molded pattern, are believed to have been made in the late 1880s period. The bells and bell covered butter dishes became very popular throughout the country. An 1889 Butler Brothers Christmas catalog showed a smaller bell with the same pattern.

Pottery and Glassware Reporter
November 18, 1886
"The Co-operative Flint Glass Co., Beaver Falls are very busy. They have out a new butter dish, appropriately called the 'Bell'. The lid of this is a real bell made of glass, with a metal clapper. It could be used to notify the household that their refection is ready, as well as to restrain their anecdotal faculties within the range of modern bounds. There is already an immense demand for this novel dish which is otherwise very handsomely got up, and the company seems to have made a ten strike in its production."

Pottery and Glassware Reporter
January 6, 1887
Reporting on the Co-operative Flint Glass Co., Beaver Falls, line of samples at the Monongahela House, Pittsburgh.
"We should not forget to mention the bell butter dish lately produced at this factory and which has had an immense sale. The cover of the dish is a glass bell with a metal clapper, and it answers all the purposes of a bronze or brass one. It is entirely out of the common run of things and its sale will undoubtedly keep up until every family in the country has one."

Crockery & Glass Journal
March 17, 1887
Reporting on the Co-operative Flint Glass Co., Beaver Falls.
"They got out this spring a butter dish with a cover in the form of a glass bell – a real bell with metal clapper, and emitting a clear and sonorous sound – and it has taken like wildfire with the trade."

The American Potter and Illuminator
Volume VII, No. 3, February 1888
This issue carried two illustrated advertisements, one for pressed glass bells and the other for a pressed glass covered butter dish.

GLASS BELLS, a real glass bell with tongue and made in fancy colors. size of regular hand bell, strong enough to stand usage. Put up one dozen assorted in pasteboard partition box. Put on your counter will sell at sight for 10 cents each.......... £.J

Figure 1. Two advertisements from the February 1888 issue of The American Potter and Illuminator, Volume VII, No.3. Note that the butter dishes and bells were available in crystal, amber, and blue glass.

Common to both size bells is a flat bottom metal clapper on a stiff wire held to the glass by a wire in a cork embedded in a hole formed on the inside top of the bell. Occasionally, the clapper is a round metal ball.

Blue and clear Currier & Ives pressed glass butter dishes with an open lattice base. 9" height. $75-90 each.

6.9" high bells in amber, crystal, and blue glass. The pattern is #130, Currier & Ives. The clapper is held by a wire attached to the glass by a cork embedded in the glass. $60-70 each.

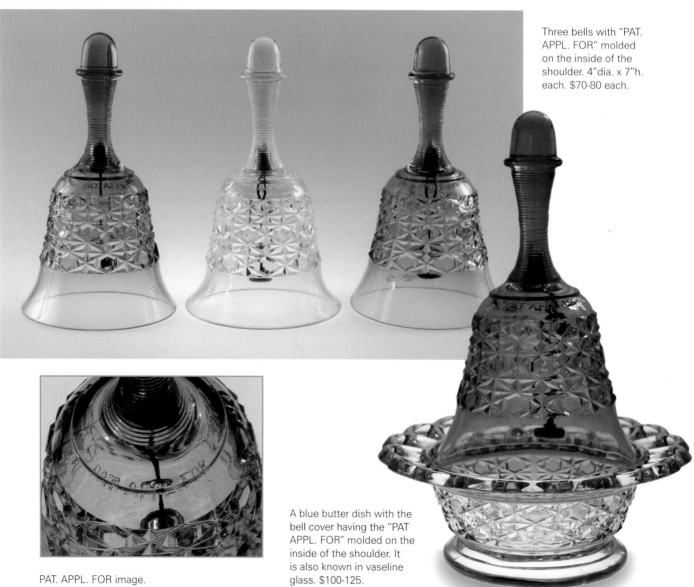

Three bells with "PAT. APPL. FOR" molded on the inside of the shoulder. 4"dia. x 7"h. each. $70-80 each.

PAT. APPL. FOR image.

A blue butter dish with the bell cover having the "PAT APPL. FOR" molded on the inside of the shoulder. It is also known in vaseline glass. $100-125.

The smaller pattern bells, 2.75"dia. x 5"h. each.
$50-60 each.

All the bells are three molded Currier & Ives pattern design. The pattern is named after a star and dot pattern seen on the rim of the company's balky mule plate showing a mule pulling a cart stalled on a railroad track with a train approaching. It's a scene similar to the type seen on some Currier & Ives plates. The pattern was also known as No.130 and Eulalia.

In 1976, a bell collector had the Currier and Ives pattern butter dishes in crystal, amber, blue, and vaseline. They also had a base in cobalt blue glass. All the bells had the molded PAT. APPL. FOR on the inside shoulder of the bell. The author has searched hundreds of patents from 1876 to 1891, but no patent for the bell or butter dishes has been found to date.

An 1889 Butler Brothers Christmas catalog advertisement shows the smaller bell.

A metal hook was used to attach the smaller bell to another item. These smaller bells have a small indentation for the hook on opposite sides at the top of the handle. $60-70.

Damron's Glass Engraving
Sisterville, West Virginia, 1922 -1966

Damron Alpine
Glass Engraving
Helen, Georgia, 1966-

Damron's makes a variety of hand engraved glassware including some bells. Some bells have been engraved to commemorate events and as souvenirs.

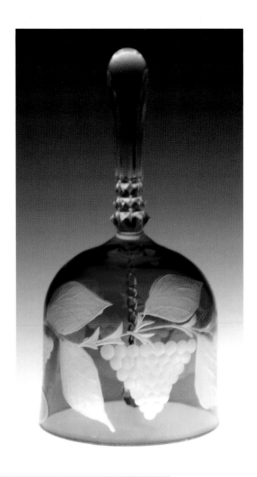

A Damron's blown cranberry glass bell with engraved grapes decoration and clear colorless handle. 3.25"dia. x 6.5"h. $25-35.

Two Damron's blown glass bells. The bell on the left is green glass with clear colorless glass handle and engraved "Kimball, MN, 1886-1986", 2.9"dia. x 5.25"h. The bell on the right is cranberry glass with clear colorless handle and engraved grapes decoration. 2.75"dia. x 5"h. $25-30 each.

Disney

A series of Disney princess bells. The boxes for the bells state that the porcelain figurines were made in Japan and the crystal bell was made and assembled in the USA. The maker is unknown to the author.

Four Disney princess series bells. Top left: Sleeping Beauty, 2.6"dia. x 5.25"h. Top right: Cinderella, 2.6"dia. x 5"h. Lower left: Snow White, 2.6"dia. x 5"h. Lower right: Jasmine, 2.6"dia. x 4.75"h. $30-40 each.

Enesco Corporation
Elk Grove, Illinois, 1959-

Enesco Corporation started in 1958 as the import division of N. Shure Company. Under several owners for several years, the company was sold in 1983 as a subsidiary of Stanhome, Inc. In 1998 Stanhome, Inc. was renamed Enesco Group, Inc. The company distributes a wide variety of products under the Enesco name. Glass bells are known to have been made for the company in subsidiaries in Germany and Japan.

A pressed floral pattern in clear glass with a three part golden handle made by Annahutte, Germany, for Enesco. c.1987. 2.75"dia. x 4.75"h. $20-25.

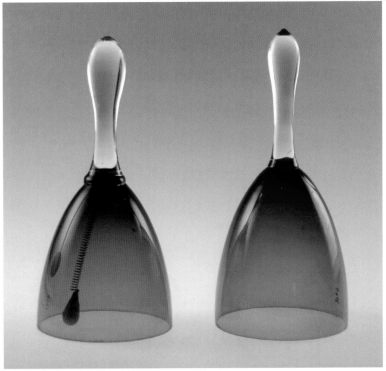

A pair of blown clear glass bells made in Japan for Enesco. 2.9"dia. x 6.25"h. $20-25 each.

Erskine Glass Company
Wellsburg, West Virginia, 1919-1987

The original wares of the company were lamps and novelty items. Later the company made illuminating glassware for the lamp and lighting fixture industry and private mold items. Some bells were made for the American Bicentennial.

An Erskine milk glass bell with bronze handle and with a sepia US seal and eagle painted by Fabian. 3.5"dia. x 4.1"h. $25-30.

Two Erskine Bicentennial blown glass bells. The bell on the left is dark blue with a ship outline, horizontal rings, and dates in the underlying frosted glass. The bell on the right is cream colored with painted red Colonial soldier and with dates and horizontal circles in blue. Both have a bronze handle and a round wood ball clapper. 3.4"dia. x 4"h. each. $25-30 each.

Fenton Art Glass Company
Williamstown, West Virginia, 1905-

The Fenton Art Glass Company over many years has produced many glass bells in a variety of patterns. In 2005 they celebrated their centennial and produced several bells to celebrate. They have been the most prolific producer of glass bells in the world. In this section are presented Fenton bells from the author's collection and parts of the collections of two other bell collectors.

A Fenton clear colorless hobnail glass bell with tapered notched square handle and a metal clapper on a thin wire. It was sold by Fenton with a label dated 1-9-67. 3"dia. x 5.6"h. $40-50.

An early Fenton clear Daisy Cut glass bell with an etched "Bell is ringing for you at 121 & 123 Main St." along the rim. 2.6"dia. x 5.9"h. $45-60.

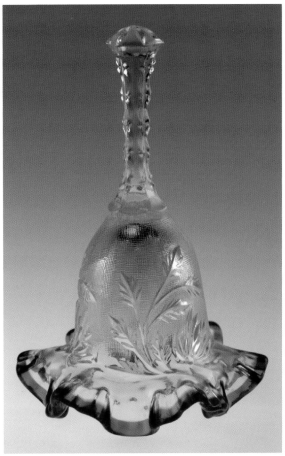

A Fenton blue glass bell with ruffled rim and a molded "Wildflower" pattern, mold 4560. c.1999. 4.6"dia. x 6.9"h. $50-60.

A Fenton ruby glass bell with a "Star Bright" decoration by C. A. Hall, 2005. Mold 7768SQ. 4.25"dia. x 6.75"h. $50-60.

A Fenton lavender glass bell with a black ruffled rim. 4.75"dia. x 6.75"h. $50-60.

A Fenton Marigold glass bell in a daisy and button pattern with an amber ribbed glass handle. Mold 1966. 4"dia. x 5.9"h. $35-50.

A Fenton violet glass bell with painted yellow flowers in an oval shape. 2.5" x 1.75" x 4.4"h. $40-55.

A Fenton clear glass bell with a painted violet decoration by S. Miller. 2.4"dia. x 4.4"h. $35-50.

A Fenton violet aubergine colored glass bell with a floral decoration in an oval shape. 2.5" x 1.75" x 4.25"h. $45-60.

A Fenton amethyst carnival glass bell decorated in a "Star Bright" pattern by Brenda Williams in 2005, the Fenton Centennial. Mold 4764UN. 4.25"dia. x 5.5"h. $50-60.

A Fenton opal mist glass bell in an oval shape and decorated with a "Chickadees in Snow" pattern by Christy Riggs during the Fenton Centennial in 2005. Mold 7566R2. 4" x 3" x 7h. $60-70.

A Fenton purple and white slag glass hobnail pattern bell made for Levay in 1980. 3"dia. x 5.75"h. $30-45.

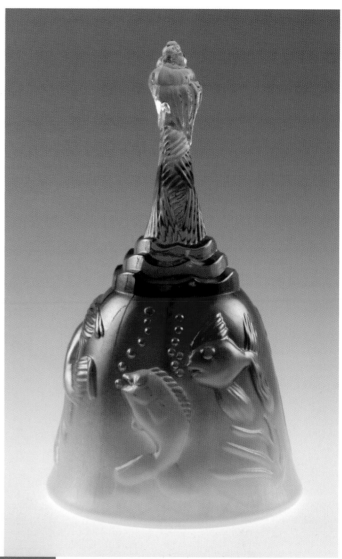

A Fenton clear purple glass bell with flower painted by A. Farley. 2.1"dia. x 3.5"h. $35-40.

A Fenton frosted white and gold glass bell with molded fish decoration. 4"dia. x 6.75"h. $50-60.

Two Fenton bells in clear pink and colorless glass with scalloped rim and painted flowers. Signed M. Kibbe and M. Young. 2"dia. x 4.5"h. $35-40 each.

Two Fenton pink clear glass "Madras" bells with painted floral decoration by M. Kibbe. 2"dia. x 4.5"h. $35-45 each.

A Fenton opal glass bell with a painted floral scene. 2.4"dia. x 4.25"h. $35-45.

Two Fenton bells in black glass with identical painted floral decoration. 4"dia. x 6.75"h. and 2.4"dia. x 4.4"h. $50-70 and $35-50.

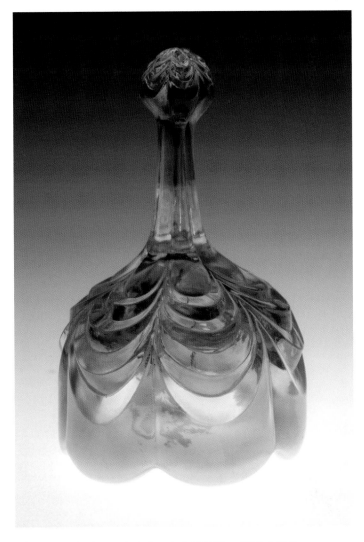

A Fenton opal mist carnival glass bell. 6536NI. c.2005. 3.5"dia. x 6.25"h. $40-50.

A Fenton frosted yellow daisy & button glass bell. 4"dia. x 6.5"h. $60-70.

Presented next are Fenton bells from the collection of Jo Ann Thompkins.

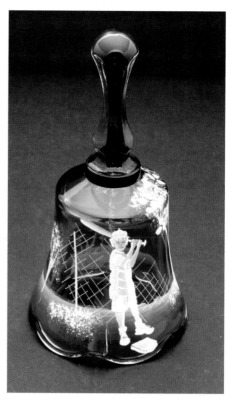

A Fenton Daisy & Button iridized teal glass bell made for Gracious Touch in 1988. 3.3"dia. x 5.75"h. $35-45.

A Fenton Daisy & Button iridized ruby glass bell. 200 were made for Sage Allen in the 1970s. 3"dia. x 6"h. $35-45.

A Fenton violet glass bell with a boy at bat, named "Batter Up", made in 2006 as part of a Four Seasons Bell Collection. #7668FX designed by Robin Spindler. 3.25"dia. x 6.5"h. $55-65.

A Fenton crystal clear glass bell with blistered interior and painted with floral and fruit design. #1765 made in 1993. 3.25"dia. x 6.25"h. $75-85.

A pair of Fenton Pennsylvania Dutch designs painted on opal glass in 2004. The left bell, #2976H5, is 3.25"dia. x 6.6"h. $40-50. The right bell, #2768H55, is 2.1"dia. x 4.5"h. $30-35.

A Fenton opal satin glass bell, called "Majestic Flight". #7667EE designed by Beverly Cumberledge. The bell is part of a Designer Series. 1200 made in 1984. 3.5"dia. x 6"h. $100-125.

A pair of Fenton glass bells. The left bell, #7564, is custard glass with a scalloped bottom edge. The edge and handle have been painted light pink. The robins and flowers were painted by Louise Piper in 1979. 3.5"dia. x 6"h. $50-60. The right bell, #7667 and dated 3/8/84, is milk glass painted in pink luster with an apple blossoms design. 3.5"dia. x 6"h. $65-75.

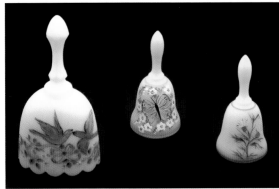

These three Fenton bells are painted by Louise Piper. The left bell is a 1985 oval satin glass bell with painted bluebirds. 3.5" x 2.5" x 6.5"h. $60-70. The center bell is a custard petite bell, #7564, painted with butterflies and carnations on one side and carnations on the other side. The bell was made for FAGCA in 1985. 2.25"dia. 4.5"h. $35-45. The right bell is custard glass with painted flowers, c.1986. 2.25"dia. x 4.5"h. $35-45.

A Fenton cobalt blue glass bell with children painted March 1, 1983 by Louise Piper. The inside of the bell has a diamond optic design. 3.25"dia. x 6.75"h. $50-60.

Fenton made a series of bells for the Longaberger Basket Company, Dresden, OH. The four diamond optic bells show Longaberger baskets with the color of the arrangements matching the color of the crimped bottom edge of the bell. Left to right, the first bell in pink, with 1998 on the back and noting their 25th anniversary, followed by 1999 in blue, 2000 in lavender, and 2001 in green. 3.4"dia. x 6.6"h. each. The first three bells were painted by V. L. Anderson and the last by S. Massey. $60-75 each.

A Fenton opal satin glass bell painted with a house and yellow ribbon on a tree in honor of men and women who served their country. #7668YQ. 1,000 made. Painted by Ann Farley in 1991. 3.5"dia. x 6"h. Rare. $300-350.

The back of the bell has printed on it "In honor of our men and women who served their country well for a peaceful world."

Three Fenton bells. Left to right: a Medallion bell mold in Burmese glass. Each oval has painted flowers by Lissa Lucas with the addition of a butterfly in one oval. 3.5"dia. x 6.75"h. $40-50. The center bell is Atlantis in Burmese glass painted by D. Brunn and made for QVC. 4"dia. x 6.5"h. $65-75. The right bell is Blue Burmese, also for QVC, with painted pansy design by B. Fluharty. 3.5"dia. x 5.6"h. $65-75.

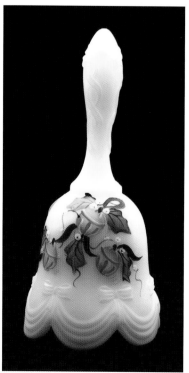

A Fenton Roselene Drapery made in 2009 for QVC. A painted "Fenton USA" is on one of the bottom scalloped edges. 3"dia. x 6"h. $50-60.

A Fenton Medallion mold Burmese glass bell with painted flowers by Diane Barbour in 2003. There are small white frit berries on the design. 3.1"dia. x 6.6"h. $55-65.

A Fenton milk glass Paisley mold glass bell with a ruby stripe inner rim. 4.5"dia. x 7.25"h. c.1993. $65-75.

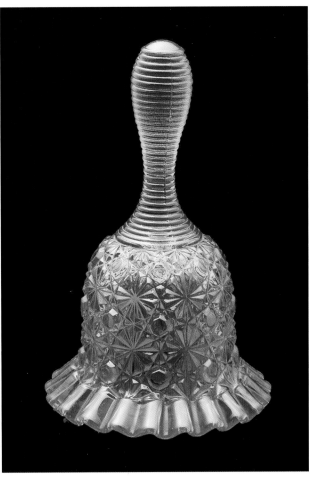

A Fenton Aqua Marigold iridescent Atlantis bell made for QVC in 1995. 4"dia. x 6.5"h. $50-60.

A Fenton orange daisy and button glass bell with a stiff wire and lead sinker type clapper. 3.6"dia. x 5.75"h. $40-50.

A Fenton mulberry blown glass bell with applied colorless handle. 3.1"dia. x 6.25"h. $85-95.

A Fenton Dave Fetty 2005 creation in a ruby and milk glass design. 3.6"dia. x 6.1"h. $120-130.

A Fenton Dave Fetty 2008 creation in cobalt blue over milk glass with painted black hanging hearts design. 3.75"dia. x 5.75"h. $110-120.

A Fenton daisy and button iridescent amethyst carnival glass bell. 3.6"dia. x 5.75"h. $50-60.

Three Fenton 2009 glass bells. Left to right: a key lime bell for QVC painted with a floral decoration by J. K. Spindler. 4.5"dia. x 6.75"h. $65-75; center plum glass bell with butterfly design painted by J. K. Spindler. 3"dia. x 6"h. $55-65; Blue Lagoon Whispers bell painted by J. Cutshaw. 4.5"dia. x 6"h. $50-60.

A cameo satin glass Fenton bell originally called Dogwood although a dogwood flower only has four petals. This sample bell, which has five petals, was redone later with four petals. 3.1"dia. x 6.25"h. $50-60.

Two rare Fenton custard glass bells with decorated design called The General. The larger bell is 3.6"dia. x 5.5"h. $210-230. The smaller bell is 2.25"dia. x 4.5"h. $50-60.

A 1983 Fenton bell in cameo satin glass, #7564TT, created by Michael Dickenson and painted by J. Brown. 3.4"dia. x 6.25"h. $50-60.

Two Fenton Favrene glass bells. The left bell, #7746YE, called Magical Meadows, with a sand carved design of horses, is one of four bells in the designer series in 2002 by Robin Spindler. 1500 made. 3"dia. x 6.5"h. $80-90. The bell on the right in a Spanish Lace mold is a sample bell from 1984. 3.6"dia. x 5.9"h. $60-70.

A Fenton lavender, white, and plum Paisley 1993 bell. 4.5"dia. x 6.6"h. $75-90.

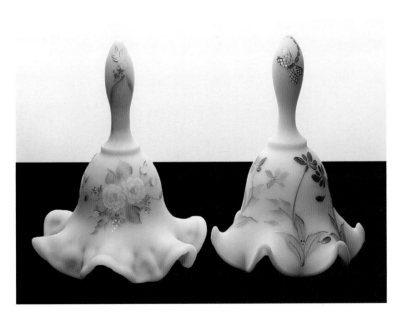

Two Fenton bells. The left bell is Blue Burmese glass and one of 98 made for Mary Walwrath in 2000 as part of a series called Circle of Love. 4"dia. x 6"h. $75-90. The second bell is Lotus Mist Green glass, called Morning Peace, #1127-1H, and one of 1500 in a 2001 designer series, was designed by Robin Spindler and painted by Susan Fluharty. 4"dia. x 6"h. $60-70.

Two Fenton glass bells, #17536, painted by D. Anderson with a rock scene on the left bell and trees on the right bell. 3"dia. x 6"h. each. $30-40 each.

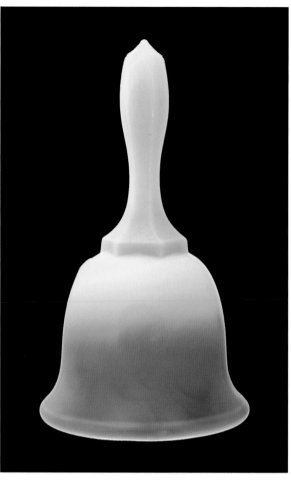

A Fenton roselene Paisley glass bell painted by D. Cutshaw in 1991. One of 200 made. 3.1"dia. x 6.6"h. $80-90.

A Fenton Burmese glass bell from 1982. 3.6"dia. x 6"h. $50-60.

Opposite:
A Fenton chocolate glass daisy and button pattern bell with a ribbed handle. 4"dia. x 6.75"h. $80-90.

Far right:
A Fenton chocolate glass bell in the Whitton pattern. It is signed 'Fenton USA' on a portion of the shoulder. 4.5"dia. x 6.25"h. $80-90.

Three Fenton bells. The left bell is Peking Blue glass in the Syndenham mold. 4"dia. x 6.25"h. $45-60. The center bell is of cameo opalescent glass with a vine pattern. 3.9"dia. x 5.6"h. $40-50. The bell on the right is of jade green glass in a Lily of the Valley mold. 3.9"dia. x 5.25"h. $40-50.

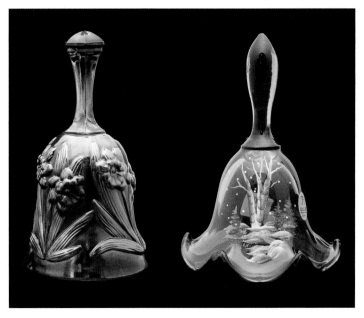

A pair of Fenton bells. The left bell, #8660Z5, is of marigold carnival with an indigo blue handle and molded iris design. 3.4"dia. x 6"h. $60-70. The bell on the right, #7768KH, from the Christmas 2007 supplement, is in indigo blue glass with a birch tree in winter painted by Ann Farley. 4"dia. x 6"h. $60-70.

A Fenton milk glass bell designed by Louise Piper in 1987 with a country scene painted by Linda Evans. 3.5"dia. x 5.4"h. $65-75.

Presented next are some bells from the collection of Mary and Ken Moyer.

Fenton glass bell samples of one-of-a-kind marble design. 3.25"dia. x 6.5"h. $60-70 each.

A Fenton Indigo Marigold carnival Daffodil glass bell with blue handle. #8660-Z5. 2008 Limited edition. 3.5"dia. x 6.25"h. $55-65.

A Fenton blue glass bell with an ivory ruffled rim and colored flower and stars decoration made for sale on QVC. C23197. Signed Gilbert Tapia. 4.5"dia. x 6.75"h. $50-60.

A Fenton sample glass bell in purple glass with ruffled rim and a milk glass twisted design handle. 3.75"dia. x 7"h. $70-80.

Presented next are bells from the collection of Mary and Ken Moyer that were decorated by Julie Martin of Ephrata, Pennsylvania.

Julie Martin is a self-taught artist whose mother and grandmother were artists. She paints on almost any medium. She started painting on glass bells about twenty years ago using glass blanks primarily from Fenton, but also some from Pilgrim, Westmoreland, and West Virginia companies. The bells shown here are one-of-kind painted over the years primarily on Fenton blanks for Ken and Mary Moyer. All the bells are signed "Julie".

An opal iridescent Fenton bell blank painted with a Monarch Butterfly and Thistle Flowers. 4.5"dia. x 6.5"h. $55-65.

A Burmese Fenton glass bell blank painted with Pansy pattern. 4.75"dia. x 7"h. $55-65.

A frosted yellow Fenton bell blank painted with a "Wilkum" sign. 4"dia. x 6"h. $55-65.

A clear pink Fenton bell blank painted with a Church in Winter scene. 4.5"dia. x 7"h. $55-65.

A Fenton frosted green glass bell blank painted with a Colorado Mountain scene. 3.75"dia. x 6.5"h. $55-65.

A Fenton Burmese glass bell blank painted with a Monarch Butterfly. 4.5"dia. x 7"h. $55-65.

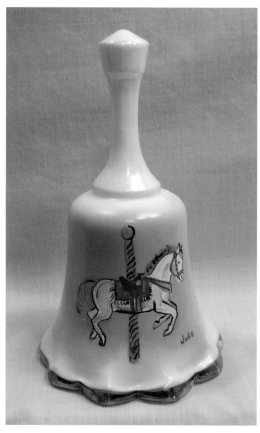

A Fenton amber glass bell blank painted with a Kitten. 3.75" x 6.5"h. $55-65.

A Fenton ivory glass bell blank painted with a Carousel. 4.5"dia. x 7"h. $55-65.

A Fenton black glass bell blank painted with a
Snowman. 4" x 6.75"h. $55-65.

A Fenton blue glass bell blank painted with a Three Wise
Men scene. 3.5" x 6.5"h. $55-65.

A Fenton black glass bell blank painted with a Horse
and Sleigh winter scene. 3.5" x 6.5"h. $55-65.

A Fenton clear glass bell blank painted with a Cabin in the Mountains scene. 3.5"dia. x 6.5"h. $55-65.

A Fenton ivory colored glass bell blank with a painted Pig and Whistle. 3.75"dia. x 3.75"h. $55-65.

A Fenton clear blue glass bell blank with a painted Girl Picking Flowers. 4" x 6.75"h. $55-65.

A Fenton clear red glass bell blank painted with a Swan. 4" x 7"h. $55-65.

A Fenton clear red glass bell blank painted with a Polar Bear. 4" x 7"h. $55-65.

A Fenton clear red glass bell blank painted with a Girl Blowing Bubbles. 4" x 7"h. $55-65.

A Fenton amber glass bell blank painted with a Sled Ride. 4" x 6.75"h. $55-65.

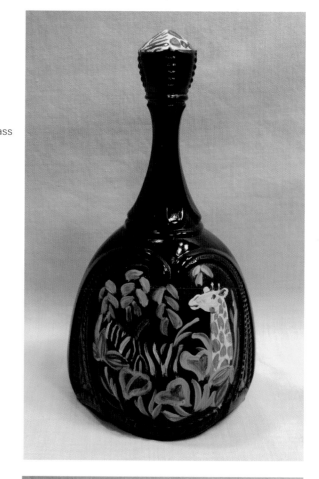

A Fenton black glass bell blank painted with a Midnight Safari scene. 4" x 6.75"h. $55-65.

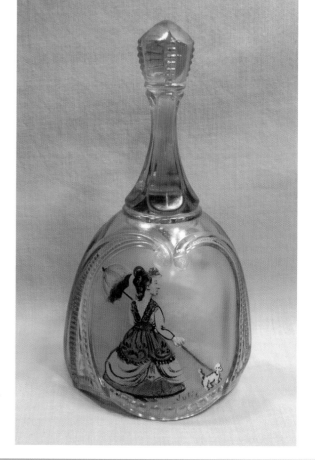

A Fenton amber glass bell blank painted with a Southern Belle Walking a Dog. 4" x 6.75"h. $55-65.

A Fenton ivory glass bell blank with a painted "Got Mail?" scene. 4"dia. x 7"h. $55-65.

A Fenton ivory glass bell blank painted with a Winter Scene. 4"dia. x 5.5"h. $55-65.

A Fenton frosted yellow glass bell blank with a painted Owl. 3.25"dia. x 6"h. $55-65.

A Fenton opal satin glass bell blank painted with a Statue of Liberty. 3.5"dia. x 6"h. $55-65.

A Fenton clear glass bell blank painted with an Eagle in the Mountains. 3.5"dia. x 6"h. $55-65.

A Fenton clear glass bell blank with a painted Lark Bunting. 3.5"dia. x 6.75"h. $55-65.

A Fenton frosted yellow glass bell blank with a painted Fox and Young. 3.5"dia. x 6.25"h. $55-65.

A Fenton clear glass bell blank with a painted Winter Cabin in the Mountains. 3"dia. x 6.75"h. $55-65.

A Fenton clear amber glass bell blank with a painted Church in Winter. 3"dia. x 6.5"h. $55-65.

A Fenton ivory glass bell blank painted with the Reading Pennsylvania Pagoda. 3"dia. x 6.5"h. $55-65.

A Fenton ruby glass bell blank painted with an Eskimo at Home. 3.5"dia. x 6.5"h. $55-65.

A Fenton ivory glass bell blank painted with a Mother Bear and Cub. 3.5"dia. x 6.25"h. $55-65.

A Fenton milk glass bell blank painted with Animals in ovals. 3.5"dia. x 6.75"h. $55-65.

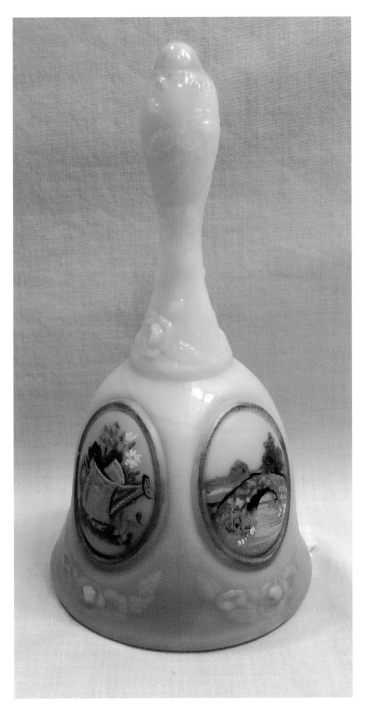

A Fenton Burmese glass bell blank painted with a Sprinkling Can and Bridge in oval views. 3.5"dia. x 6.5"h. $55-65.

A Fenton opal satin glass bell blank painted with an Outhouse. 3.5"dia. x 6"h. $55-65.

A Fenton opal satin glass bell blank painted with a House Finch. 3.5"dia. x 6"h. $55-65.

A Fenton mist green glass bell blank painted with a Hen and Chicks. 3.5"dia. x 6.5"h. $55-65.

A Fenton opal satin glass bell blank painted with a Hawaiian Lighthouse. 3.5"dia. x 6"h. $55-65.

A Fenton custard class bell blank with painted Butterfly and Flowers. 3.5"dia. x 6.75"h. $55-65.

A Fenton mist green bell blank with a painted Panda Bear. 3.5"dia. x 6"h. $55-65.

A Fenton custard glass bell blank painted with a Covered Bridge. 3.5"dia. x 6"h. $55-65.

A Fenton mist green glass bell blank with a painted Hawaiian Church. 3.5"dia. x 6.75"h. $55-65.

A Fenton Burmese satin glass bell blank with Painted Bridge and Flowers in ovals. 3.5"dia. x 6.75"h. $55-65.

A Fenton mist green glass bell blank with a painted Train. 3.5"dia. x 6"h. $55-65.

A Fenton mist green glass bell blank with a painted Ice Skating Scene. 4"dia. x 5.25"h. $55-65.

A Fenton frosted glass bell blank with painted Morning Glory. 4.5"dia. x 7"h. $55-65.

A Fenton custard satin glass bell blank painted with a Grist Mill. 4"dia. x 6.5"h. $55-65.

A Fenton clear green
glass bell blank painted
with Birds at a Feeder.
3.5"dia. x 6"h. $55-65.

A Fenton frosted custard glass bell
painted with Kittens in a Basket. 3.5"dia.
x 6.5"h. $55-65.

A Fenton clear and milk glass bell
blank with painted Humming Bird
and Fuchsia Flowers. 4.5"dia. x
6.5"h. $55-65.

A Fenton mist green glass bell blank with a painted Stage Coach. 4"dia. x 6.5"h. $55-65.

A Fenton mist green glass bell blank with a painted Covered Wagon. 4"dia. x 6.5"h. $55-65.

A Fenton frosted custard glass bell blank with a painted Irish Hay Wagon. 4"dia. x 6.5"h. $55-65.

A Fenton custard glass bell blank with a painted Raccoon Picnic. 4"dia. x 6.5"h. $55-65.

A Fenton mist green glass bell blank with a painted Sea Life. 4"dia. x 6.5"h. $55-65.

A Fenton ruby frosted and clear glass bell blank with a painted Playing with Kitten. 4"dia. x 6"h. $55-65.

A Fenton yellow aurora glass bell blank painted with a "Finch". 3.75"dia. x 7"h. $55-65.

A Fenton clear green glass bell blank with a painted Sea Life. 3.5"dia. x 6.75"h. $55-65.

A Fenton clear green glass bell blank painted with a Country Scene. 3.5"dia. x 6"h. $55-65.

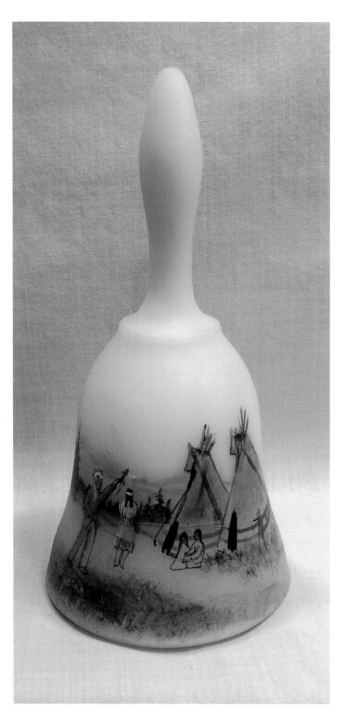

A Fenton custard glass bell blank painted with a Ring Neck Pheasant. 3.5"dia. x 6"h. $55-65.

A Fenton frosted custard glass bell blank painted with an "Indian Tee Pee" 3.5"dia. x 6.75"h. $55-65.

The next three bells were painted on blanks from Pilgrim and Westmoreland.

A Pilgrim frosted yellow glass bell blank painted with a Boy Riding a Bicycle in the snow. 3.75"dia. x 7"h. $55-65.

A Westmoreland light blue glass bell blank painted with Fruit. 3.5"dia. x 6"h. $55-65.

A Pilgrim clear glass bell blank with a painted Chicago Harbor Lighthouse. 3.75"dia. x 7"h. $55-65.

Findlay Flint Glass Company

Findlay, Ohio, August 12, 1889-June 6, 1891

During its short time of existence the Findlay Flint Glass Company produced a glass bell in a DOT pattern, also known as the Stippled Forget Me Not pattern. The bell was also used as the cover of a similar pattern butter dish.

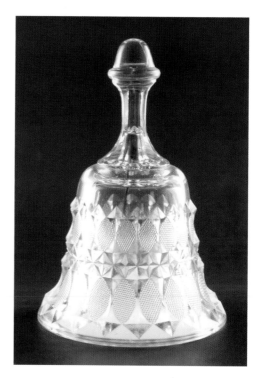

A Findlay Flint Glass Co. sugar bowl with a bell cover in a frosted leaf "DOT" pattern. 7.5"h. $110-125.

A Findlay Flint Glass Co. clear frosted leaf "DOT" pattern bell. 4"dia. x 6"h. $75-90.

Fischer Crystal Bells

Overland Park, Kansas, 1972-

Since 1975 Fischer Crystal Bells has produced glass bells primarily from imported goblets; the base is removed, the blank is decorated or etched, and a clapper is attached. The bells are sometimes signed Glen Jones.

A Fischer Crystal Bells clear crystal bell made from a Crystal d'Arques blank and etched with "A BELL FOR MOTHER". It is signed "Glen Jones" 3.6"dia x 6.75"h. $25-35.

Two signed Glen Jones bells. Left bell is frosted glass with a girl cameo and etched "My Mother's Bell" and violet handle. 2.75"dia. x 6.1"h. Right bell uses a Crystal d'Arques blank with an etched "A BELL FOR MOTHER". 3.6"dia. x 6.75"h. $30-40 each.

Fostoria Glass Company
Moundsville, West Virginia, 1891-1986

Fostoria produced pressed pattern bells and blown glass bells starting in 1971. The bell patterns usually match the pattern on other stemware items produced by the company.

A Fostoria clear glass bell with a wooden handle. 3.1"dia. x 5.75"h. $30-40.

A Fostoria clear pale violet glass bell with a four-part square handle. 2.5"dia. x 4.5"h. $35-45.

A Fostoria clear colorless glass bell with a molded twisted handle. c.1980. 3.25"dia. x 7"h. $25-35.

The Franklin Mint

Middleton, Pennsylvania, 1964-

The Franklin Mint is a private mint that has created works of fine art, objects d'art, and treasured collectibles for over 45 years. Among their products glass bells can be found with ceramic flowers and bird handles. The bells shown are from the collection of Sally & Rob Roy.

A Franklin Mint glass bell with a bunting bird handle. 3"dia. x 6.5"h. $40-50.

A pair of Franklin Mint glass bells with an indigo bunting handle on the left and a chickadee handle on the right. 3"dia. x 6.5"h. each. $40-50.

A pair of Franklin
Mint glass bells with
orchid handle on the
left and gardenia
handle on the right.
3"dia. x 6"h. each.
$40-50 each.

A pair of Franklin
Mint glass bells with
a hibiscus handle
on the left and a lily
handle on the right.
3"dia. x 6"h. each.
$40-50 each.

Glassplax, Inc.
Murrieta, California, 1984-

Glassplax is known for producing awards in the form of plaques made of crystal. One of its subsidiaries is Sperrin Crystal from County Tyrone, Northern Ireland, which produces cut glass and engraved glass items including bells. See *Glass Bells from Around the World* (Schiffer Publishing), United Kingdom, Sperrin Crystal, for one of their bells.

Guernsey Glass Company
Cambridge, Ohio, 1970-2007

The company produced smocking pattern glass bells in the 1970s using a mold from the Akro Agate Company. A "B" for Harold Bennett, the recently deceased owner, is molded on the top inside of the bell. The smocking pattern bell mold is now owned by the Wilkerson Glass Company of Moundsville, West Virginia.

A Guernsey Glass bell in a clear blue glass smocking pattern. 3.4"dia. x 5.75"h. $45-55.

A Guernsey Glass in a marbleized pink smocking pattern. 3.4"dia. x 5.75"h. $50-60.

Two Guernsey smocking pattern glass bells. The bell on the left is clear colorless glass with a red handle; the bell on the right has a marbleized dark pink color. 3.4"dia. x 5.5"h. $40-55 each.

A. H. Heisey & Company
Newark, Ohio, 1896-1957

Heisey produced some engraved glass bells and pressed molded glass bells.

A Heisey cobalt blue glass bell with a clear colorless rosette handle. The interior has 10 sides. 2.25"dia. x 3.25"h. $130-150.

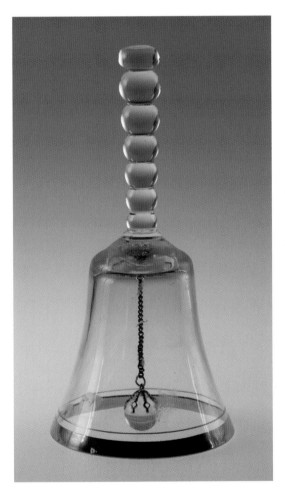

Imperial Glass Company
Bellaire, Ohio, 1901-1931

Imperial Glass Corporation
Bellaire, Ohio, 1931-1984

Starting in 1901 as the Imperial Glass Company, the firm was reorganized as the Imperial Glass Corporation in 1931. In 1973 the company was purchased by Lenox, Inc., sold in 1981 to several individuals, and was out of business in 1984. The company produced a variety of bells, but is best known for the slag glass bells produced between 1959 and 1977.

An Imperial clear glass Candlewick bell with a gold rim and 7 knop handle. c.1968. 3"dia. x 6.25"h. $30-40.

An Imperial clear glass Candlewick bell with a 4 knop handle. c.1978. 3"dia. x 5"h. $25-30.

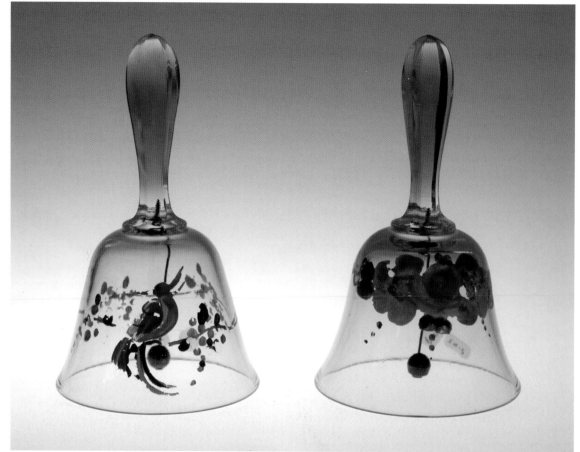

Two Imperial pink glass bells. The bell on the left is painted with a bird and flowers and the one on the right with flowers. c.1930. 3.25"dia. x 5.5"h. $30-40.

An Imperial clear pink glass bell with painted flowers and butterfly. 3.25"dia. x 5.25"h. $30-40.

An Imperial clear pink glass bell with an overlay of bronze painted flowers and foliage. 3.25"dia. x 5.25"h. $190-200.

Two Imperial clear green glass bells. The bell on the left has a decorated bird and flowers. The bell on the right is etched with "Madison 1930". 3.25"dia. x 5.5"h. $30-40 each.

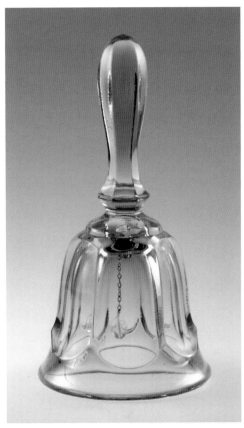

An Imperial pale brown slag glass bell. 3"dia. x 5.75"h. $25-35.

An Imperial Glass bell in yellow panels. It is an "Old Williamsburg" 1959 "Heisey by Imperial" bell. 3.25"dia. x 6.25"h. $30-40.

Levay Glass
Edwardsville, Illinois, 1984-1993

Intaglio Designs, Ltd.
Wood River, Illinois, 1993-1998

Intaglio made many small lead crystal bells with ceramic handles of animals, clowns, and dolls. Some bells have a golden heart clapper, but others have a colored multi-faceted crystal clapper. Some of the later bells are clear glass with a figured clapper. Some bells can be found with an Intaglio label.

An Intaglio Designs clear glass bell with a plastic handle of a clown playing cymbals. 2"dia. x 5"h. $25-35.

An Intaglio Designs clear glass bell with an angel as a clapper. 3"dia. x 5.5"h. $25-30.

An Intaglio Designs clear glass bell with a "Fantasy Santa" handle. 2"dia. x 4.25"h. $25-35.

An Intaglio Designs clear glass bell with a plastic handle of a clown playing a saxophone. 2"dia. x 4.75"h. $25-35.

Jefferson Glass Company
Steubenville, Ohio, 1900-1906
Follansbee, West Virginia, 1907-1930

Jefferson Glass Company is best known for bells produced from 1909 to 1915 in flashed ruby glass or custard glass with gold rims produced as souvenirs for restaurants and to commemorate special events in the United States. Bells were also produced in ruby glass and golden carnival glass without the gold rim. Similar bells were marketed and sold in South America. The mold for the bells originated in 1908 with the Ohio Flint Glass Company, Lancaster, Ohio.

In 1919, the Jefferson Glass Company sold the mold to the Central Glass Works, Wheeling, West Virginia.

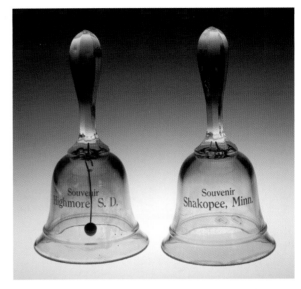

Two Jefferson Glass Co. bells in clear amber and colorless glass. The left bell is marked with "Souvenir Highmore, SD" 3.4"dia. x 6.25"h. The right bell is marked with "Souvenir Shakopee, Minn." 3.25"dia. x 6.25"h. $60-70 each.

Three Jefferson Glass Co. bells in ruby and clear glass. Some still have the gold finish on the raised rim. Left to right the bells are marked "Carlton Terrace, New York"; "Sphinx Club, New York"; and "Escuela Mixta No.2, Octubre 27 de 1912" from Uruguay. 3.25"dia. x 6.25"h. $55-70 each.

A Jefferson Glass Co. bell in clear ruby glass, gold rim, and clear colorless handle with decorated "Perry Memorial". c.1915. The memorial was established in Ohio, about 5 miles south of the Canadian border, to honor those who fought in the Battle of Lake Erie during the war of 1812. It was opened to the public on June 13, 1915. 3.25"dia. x 6.25"h. $40-50.

Lenox Group, Inc.
Edin Prairie, Minnesota, 2005-

The Lenox Group deals in tabletop, giftware, and collectibles marketed under Department 56, Lenox, Gorham, and Dansk brands. Lenox has produced bells primarily to commemorate special events and holidays.

Lenox, Incorporated
Lawrenceville, New Jersey, 1906-

Over the years Lenox acquired several firms, including Bryce Brothers. In 1976 Lenox was acquired by Department 56 and then was acquired in 1983 by the Brown-Forman Corporation. Lenox, Inc. is now a subsidiary of the Lenox Group, Inc.

A Lenox clear glass bell with a frosted bird handle and silver rim. 3.25"dia. x 8"h. $30-40.

A Lenox Imperial carnival green glass pattern 404 bell. 3.75"dia. x 6.75"h. $35-45.

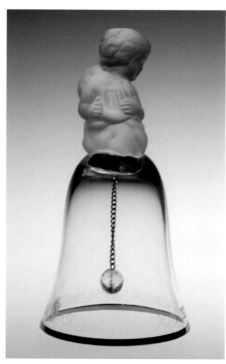

A Lenox clear glass bell with a molded frosted glass angel handle and silver rim. 3"dia. x 5.75"h. $30-40.

A Lenox 2006 annual clear glass bell with a frosted glass Snowman handle with silver ring base. Made in the Czech Republic. 2.25"dia. x 4.5"h. $25-30.

A Lenox clear glass bell with an etched sleigh ride and with a snowflake molded handle and silver rim. c.1986. 3.25"dia. x 7"h. $30-40.

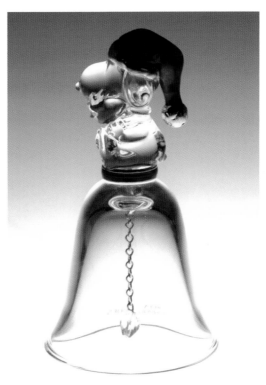

A Lenox 2003 annual clear lead crystal bell with a Peanuts Snoopy, hugging Woodstock, with red cap handle. Made in the Czech Republic. 2.4"dia. x 4.25"h. $25-30.

A Lenox clear glass bell with a cut candle pattern and partial loop handle. 1.6"dia. x 3"h. $25-30.

Libbey Glass Company
Toledo, Ohio, 1880-1935

In 1893 the Libbey Glass Company had a pavilion at the Columbian Exposition in Chicago, Illinois with the exclusive right to manufacture and sell glass at the fair. Many glass bells were produced there primarily of etched blown glass. In later years some clear glass engraved glass bells were produced.

A Libbey Glass Co. clear glass bell with etched "Worlds Fair 1893" in a circle and flowers and with a spiral twisted frosted glass handle. One of four variations of the same bell. 2.9"dia. x 4.6"h. $100-125.

A Libbey Glass Co. clear ruby glass bell with a spiral twisted clear glass handle. It is etched with "Worlds Fair 1893". 3"dia. x 4.4"h. $450-500.

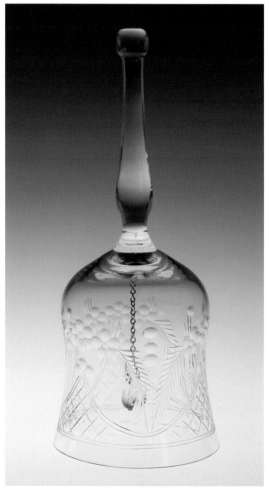

A Libbey Rock Sharp clear glass bell engraved with a floral decoration. 3"dia. x 7"h. $90-100.

Lotus Cut Glass Company
1912-1920

Lotus Glass Company, Inc.
Barnesville, Ohio, 1920-

The Lotus Glass Company decorates glass produced by other companies. Some bells can be found with the Lotus paper label still attached. Many bells were made in 1939 on eight different shapes with fifteen different decorations. Some decorations were cut and others were decorated in gold and silver.

A Lotus clear glass bell with cut wheat pattern. 2.75"dia. x 4.5"h. $30-40.

Two Lotus clear glass bells with similar gold encrusted design. 2.75"dia. x 4.2"h. and 3.1"dia. x 4.7"h. $30-40 each.

A Lotus clear glass bell with etched floral pattern. 2.9"dia. x 4.9"h. $25-30.

Lotus clear glass bells. The bell on the left is a "Cheryl" design with a cut radial fan. The bell on the right has a rose and spiral vine etched design. 3"dia. x 4.5"h. $30-40 each.

A Lotus clear glass bell with cut horizontal stripes and punties on the shoulder. 2.75"dia. x 4.5"h. $30-40.

A Lotus clear glass bell with silver bands and handle. c.1939. 2.9"dia. x 4.5"h. $30-40.

A Lotus clear glass bell with a gold floral design and horizontal gold stripes and handle. 2.9"dia. x 4.5"h. $30-40.

A Lotus clear glass bell with a gold rim. 3"dia. x 4.75"h. $20-30.

McKee Glass Company
Jeannette, Pennsylvania, 1888-1951

The company made pressed glass molded bells primarily in the "Yutec" pattern from 1905 – 1915. Many bells were made with the name of a furniture company etched along the rim.

A McKee Glass Co. clear glass bell in a "Yutec" pattern and etched ""The Braley-Grote Furn. Co., Oakland, Cal." along the rim. 2.5"dia. x 5.1"h. $40-50.

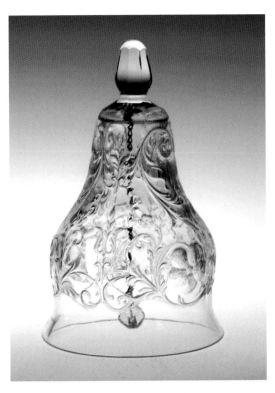

A McKee Glass Co. Prescut Rock Crystal floral pattern bell from 1942. 3.5"dia. x 5.5"h. $150-175.

A McKee Glass Co. clear glass bell in a "Yutec" pattern and etched "Compliments of The Leader Co." along the rim. 2.4"dia. x 5.25"h. $40-50.

Mid Atlantic of West Virginia, Inc.
Ellenboro, West Virginia, 1937-2006

During its many years the company produced a wide range of hand blown crystal items with some featuring floral decorations of hand cut and etched designs. A few bells are known.

Three Mid Atlantic clear colored glass bells with colorless handles. Left to right: a blue bell with etched bird and flower, 2"dia. x 4.1"h.; a pink bell with etched bird and flower, 3"dia. x 5.5"h.; a cranberry glass bell with etched flower, 1.9"dia. x 4"h. Each bell has a Mid Atlantic of West Virginia Inc. label. Each bell $20-30.

Mikasa, Inc.
Secaucus, New Jersey, 1948-

Mikasa has porcelain and glass products produced by various companies, some overseas. Glass bells with their name are known from Austria, Germany, and Slovenia.

In 2001 the company merged with J. G. Durand Industries, S. A., a parent company of Arc International and Verrerie Cristallerie d'Arques, but continues to trade under the Mikasa name.

Morgantown Glass Works
Morgantown, West Virginia, 1899-1971

Morgantown Glass Works has produced a variety of glassware including a very few bells with a golf ball stem. Bells are known in Ritz Blue and Stiegel Green glass. The company operated over the years under different names:

Economy Tumbler Co.; 1903-1923
Economy Glass Co.; 1923-1929
Morgantown Glass Works, Inc.; 1929-1937
Morgantown Glassware Guild; 1939-1971

A Morgantown Glass Works Stiegel Green glass with a colorless pressed pattern glass golf ball handle. 2.9"dia. x 4.5"h. $100-120.

Mount Washington Glass Company
New Bedford, Massachusetts, 1869-1894

Mount Washington, among its many glass products, produced glass bells in cut glass, Burmese glass, Colonial Ware, decorated white lusterless glass, and painted clear glass. Mount Washington licensed Thomas Webb & Sons to produce Burmese Glass items in England, including bells. Some Mount Washington Burmese glass bells are known that are similar to those produced in England in two parts joined by plaster and known to bell collectors as wedding bells.

In 1893, Mount Washington produced some glass articles to be sold by the Libbey Glass Company at the Columbian Exposition in Chicago. A special peachblow bell was produced at that time.

A Mt. Washington clear glass bell with painted violets and inscribed "Columbian Souvenir 1893". A two piece metal clapper with chain is attached to a twisted wire imbedded in the glass. 3.1"dia. x 4.75"h. $100-125. *Courtesy of Sally and Rob Roy.*

A Mt. Washington Glass Company peachblow mother-of-pearl satin glass bell with a diamond quilted handle and ruffled rim. Produced for the 1893 Columbian Exposition, Chicago. 4"dia. x 7"h. $600-800.

A view of the underside of the bell showing the three layers of glass.

Around 1897, the company produced some desk appointments, including some opal satin glass bells. Some other opal and clear glass bells were decorated with floral arrangements.

A Mt. Washington Glass Co. clear glass bell with a painted pansy design and twisted handle. 3.5"dia. x 5"h. $60-75.

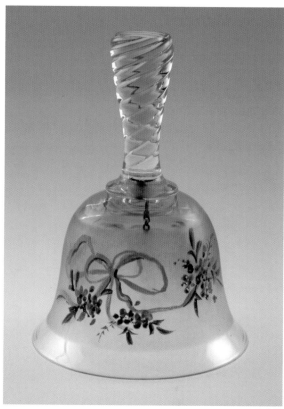

A Mt. Washington Glass Company satin glass bell with a twisted handle and arbutus flower design. c.1898. 3.1"dia. x 4.6"h. $300-400.

A Mt. Washington Glass Co. clear glass bell with painted floral decoration on a frosted glass background and a twisted handle. 3.25"dia. x 4.6"h. $65-80.

A Mt. Washington Glass Co. clear glass bell with a twisted handle. 4"dia. x 7"h. $50-60.

A Mt. Washington opal glass bell with a painted floral decoration and mottled top of handle. 2.75"dia. x 5.25"h. $200-250.

A Mt. Washington satin white glass bell with painted daisies and a two piece metal clapper with a chain attached to a twisted wire imbedded in the glass. 3.1"dia. x 5"h. $200-250. *Courtesy of Sally and Rob Roy.*

Mt. St. Helens Volcanic Ash Glass Works
Centralia, Washington, 1980-

Some glass bells have been produced using the ash resulting from recent volcanic eruptions.

A Mt. St. Helens Ash Glass bell with clear glass handle. 3.4"dia. x 9.5"h. $30-40.

A Gundersen Pairpoint peachblow glass bell with peachblow teardrop clapper. c.1953. 3"dia. x 6.4"h. $400-450.

Pairpoint Corporation/Mount Washington Glass Company
New Bedford, Massachusetts, 1894-1938

Gundersen-Pairpoint Glass Works
New Bedford, Massachusetts, 1938-1952

Gundersen Glass Works
New Bedford, Massachusetts, 1952-1957

Pairpoint Glass Company, Inc.
Spain, 1958-1970;
Sagamore, Massachusetts, 1957 and 1970-1988

Pairpoint Crystal Company, Inc.
Sagamore, Massachusetts, 1988-

Some cut glass bells were made by Pairpoint in the early 1900s, but most Pairpoint bells have been made of blown glass since 1970 with a few made during the earlier Gundersen years. Most of the recent bells are signed with a P in a diamond.

A Pairpoint dark red glass bell with clear colorless handle made for the American Bell Association 2007 convention. 3"dia. x 6.25"h. $50-60.

A Pairpoint teal glass bell with painted bird and wreath. 4"dia. x 7"h. $90-110.

A Pairpoint teal glass bell with painted flowers. 4"dia. x 7.25"h. $90-110.

A Pairpoint blue milk glass bell with pale blue swirls. 3.75"dia. x 6.75"h. $100-125.

A Pairpoint clear blue glass bell with a painted winter scene. 3.75"dia. x 6.5"h. $70-80.

A Pairpoint Burmese glass bell with a yellow glass loop handle. 3.6"dia. x 4.9"h. $175-200.

A Pairpoint clear lavender glass bell with white Nailsea striping and a 5 knop clear glass handle with twisted white ribbon. 5.25"dia. x 11.1"h. $275-300.

A Pairpoint Burmese glass bell with a yellow glass handle. 3.25"dia. x 5.75"h. $250-275.

A Pairpoint clear cranberry glass bell with a clear colorless handle with pink and white swirls and 6 knops. 5.4"dia. x 11.5"h. $250-300.

A Pairpoint rose colored glass bell with painted flower and butterfly and a 6 knop clear handle with white swirls. One of 25 made for the Pairpoint Collectors Club in 2007. 5"dia. x 11.25"h. $275-325.

A Pairpoint twisted latticino design multi-color glass bell with black handle. 3.75"dia. x 7.75"h. $150-175. *Courtesy of Mary & Ken Moyer.*

Opposite:
A pair of Pairpoint light blue glass bells with painted bird, nest, and butterflies. Clear 6 knop handle with white twisted ribbon on the larger bell. One pair of 25 made by Eileen Alletta Neary. Signed Eileen. 5.25"dia. x 12"h. and 3.4"dia x 6.5"h. $275-325 and $175-225.

A clear colorless Pairpoint glass bell with a green rim, cut wild rose decoration, white ribbons in the 4 knop handle, and a clear teardrop handle. 5"dia. x 11.75"h. $250-275. *Courtesy of Sally & Rob Roy.*

A Pairpoint yellow and white glass bell with a latticino clear glass 6 knop handle. 5.1"dia. x 10.75"h. $300-325. *Courtesy of Marilyn Grismere.*

A Pairpoint red and white diamond pattern glass bell with latticino 6 knop handle. 5"dia. x 11.5"h. $200-250. *Courtesy of Marilyn Grismere.*

A Pairpoint purple glass bell with decoration and clear glass latticino 6 knop handle. 5.5"dia. x 11"h. $300-350. *Courtesy of Marilyn Grismere.*

A Pairpoint clear glass bell with blue splattered base and latticino red and white 6 knop handle. 4"dia. x 11.4"h. $250-300. *Courtesy of Marilyn*

Pilgrim Glass Corporation
Ceredo, West Virginia, 1949-2001

Pilgrim Glass made a variety of glass bells during its half century of production. Some of the bells shown are two part bells that were made in colored cut to clear glass. Others are sand carved bells made by Kelsey Murphy when she was at Pilgrim.

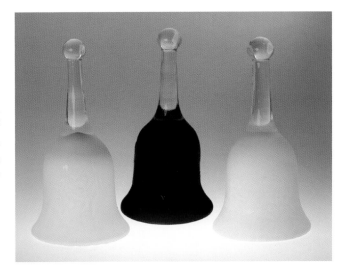

Three Pilgrim sand carved glass bells with clear colorless handles. All are signed Kelsey/Pilgrim GS5074 1997. Left to right: White Ice Skaters; Blue Bluebells; White Sleigh Ride. 3.9"dia. x 7.5"h. $75-100 each.

Three Pilgrim frosted cut to clear glass bells. Left to right: green oak leaves pattern; pink rose pattern; and amber deer pattern. 4"dia. x 7.5"h. $90-100 each.

Four Pilgrim sand carved cranberry glass bells with clear colorless handles. All are signed Kelsey/Pilgrim GS5000 2001. Left to right: Lady Cameo; Birds; Angel, Tree, & Cross; Horses & Tree. 4"dia. x 7.75"h, $150-175 each.

Pisello Art Glass Company
LaPorte, Indiana, 1982-1988

The company produced pressed glass items in limited quantities. Tina molded glass bells were made for Pisello by the Summit Art Glass Company in 1985. The number of Tina bells made is as follows: Tangerine – 256; Cobalt blue – 199; Morning Glory (light blue) – 160.

The bells were created from a mold similar to that of a perfume bottle made for Babs Creations, Inc. to commemorate the opening of the movie Gone With The Wind in 1939.

A pair of Pisello Art Glass bells in tangerine and blue glass. The tangerine bell has a "P" on the back rim. They have a clear glass ball clapper on a chain. 1.4" x 1.8" x 3.5"h. $25-40.

A 1939 Babs Creations, Inc. perfume bottle made to commemorate the movie "Gone With The Wind". A mold for the bottle was used by the Summit Art Glass Co. to make the bells for Pisello.

Queen Lace Crystal Corporation
New York, New York, 1960-

The company has had cut and copper wheel engraved glass items made in Czechoslovakia and Germany. During the 1970s engraved glass bells were made as part of the American Wildlife Series.

A Queen's Lace clear glass bell with cut hobstars and a tapered hexagonal handle. Made in Czechoslovakia for the company. 2.6"dia. x 5"h. $50-60.

A Queen's Lace glass bell with engraved bird. 2.6"dia. x 7.5"h. $50-60.

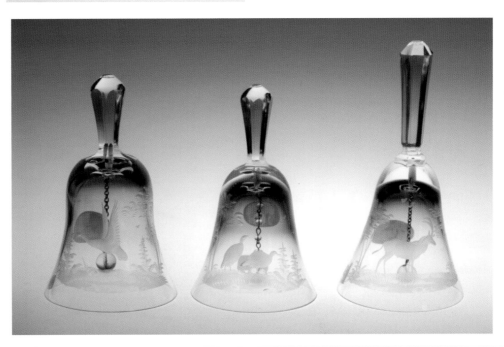

Three Queen's Lace glass bells engraved, left to right, with a flying duck, 3"dia. x 5"h.; quail, 2.9"dia. x 4.75"h.; and deer, 2.9"dia. x 5.75"h. $30-45 each.

Ron Hinkle Glass

Buckhannon, West Virginia, 1994-

Ronald L. Hinkle started a glass studio in January 1994 producing vases, bowls, and novelty figurines including animals, fruit, and flowers. A variety of bells have been produced in recent years. He has produced some bells by turning wines upside down, modifying the handle, and adding a clapper. The bells are usually signed Ron Hinkle with the year they were made. The company is also known as Hinkle's Dying Art Glassworks.

Ron Hinkle also co-operated with Kelsey Murphy and Robert Bomkamp to provide the base cameo bells which were then carved by Murphy and Bomkamp. See the Studios of Heaven section in Chapter 1.

A Ron Hinkle bell in multicolored swirls and Burmese glass handle. Signed Ron Hinkle 2008. 3.75"dia. x 6.5"h. $65-75. *Courtesy of Mary & Ken Moyer.*

Four Ron Hinkle bells in blue, green, lavender, and pink iridescent mottled glass with clear round top of handle. The green bell is signed Ron Hinkle 2005; the 3 others are signed Ron Hinkle 2006. 4"dia. x 7.5"h. $50-60 each.

Two Ron Hinkle bells in amber and blue iridescent mottled glass with a loop handle. The left bell is signed Ron Hinkle 2005 and the right bell is signed Ron Hinkle 2004. 3.5"dia. x 4.5"h. and 3.6"dia. x 5"h. $35-45 each.

A Ron Hinkle Burmese glass bell with a swirled pattern base. Signed Ron Hinkle 2008. 3.5"dia. x 7"h. $60-70. *Courtesy of Mary & Ken Moyer.*

A Ron Hinkle bell in mottled gold with clear round top of handle. Clapper is attached by a cork in the hollow handle. Signed Ron Hinkle 2008. 3.6"dia. x 7"h. $40-60. *Courtesy of Mary & Ken Moyer.*

A Ron Hinkle purple spackled glass bell with a yellow glass handle. Signed Ron Hinkle 2008. 3.25"dia. x 6"h. $50-60. *Courtesy of Mary & Ken Moyer.*

Seneca Glass Company
Morgantown, West Virginia, 1891-1983

Many bells in blown clear glass with cut designs were made primarily between 1975 and 1983. While most Seneca bells are made of clear colorless glass, some are known in red, moss green, blue, silver plate, gold plate, and frosted white glass. Known bell sizes include: 2-1/4", 3-3/4", 4-1/4", 4-1/2", 5-1/2" and 6-1/2" high.

A Seneca clear glass bell in a cut 1434 Heirloom pattern. 3.4"dia. x 6.5"h. $50-60.

A Seneca clear glass bell in a cut 1449, Tapestry pattern. 3.1"dia. x 5.5"h. $30-40.

A Seneca Olympia clear glass bell with a platinum rim. 3.25"dia. x 5.6"h. $30-40.

A Seneca clear glass bell with a silver rim. 2.5"dia. x 4.5"h. $25-35.

A Seneca clear glass bell cut in the Celeste pattern. c.1979. 2.5"dia. x 4.5"h. $30-40.

A Seneca clear glass bell cut in the Holiday pattern. c.1979. 2.1"dia. x 4.5"h. $30-40.

Sickles Glass Cutting Company

Bellaire, Ohio
St. Clairesville, Ohio, -1995

Sickles cut glass blanks for many companies including Fostoria and Imperial. A few blown cut glass bells by the company are known.

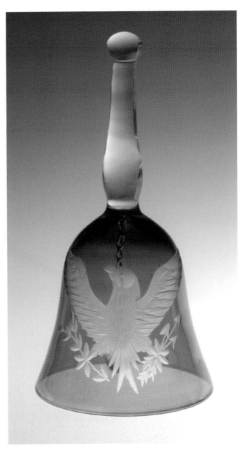

A Sickles blue cut to clear glass bell with a grape pattern and round clear colorless handle. 3.1"dia. x 6"h. $25-30.

A Sickles blue clear glass bell with engraved American eagle. 3.1"dia. x 6.1"h. A stamped 'S' in a circle is on the inside. $25-30.

Smith's Old Timer Glass

Fort Smith, Arkansas, 1960-1976

This glass factory produced many blown glass bells usually with a cork in a hollow handle to hold glass teardrop clappers.

A group of 27 Smith's Old Timer glass bells in various sizes and colors. $40-60 each. *Courtesy of Mary and Ken Moyer.*

A Smith's Old Timer clear glass bell with multi-colored swirls. 3.9"dia. x 7"h. $40-50. *Courtesy of Mary & Ken Moyer.*

L. E. Smith
Glass Company

Mt. Pleasant, Pennsylvania, 1907-

L. E. Smith has made many pressed glass items including some bells.

An L. E. Smith clear pink pressed glass bell with the painted floral "Victorian Classic" No. 300k pattern. 3.5"dia. x 6.4"h. $25-35.

An L. E. Smith clear yellow pressed glass bell with painted floral "Victorian Classic" pattern. 3.6"dia. x 6.25"h. $25-35.

Summit Art Glass Company
Ravenna, Ohio, 1972-2005

The Summit Art Glass Co. produced bells from molds that were acquired from other companies. Many bells are marked with a "V" in a circle for Russ Vogelson, the owner.

A pair of Summit Art Glass Co. bells in a blue "Wildflower" pattern with different handles. 3.1"dia. x 5.8"h. $35-40 each.

A Summit glass bell in a green slag glass "Wildflower" pattern. 3.1"dia. x 5.75"h. $30-35.

A Summit glass bell in a chocolate and orange slag glass "Wildflower" pattern. 3.1"dia. x 5.75"h. $35-45.

A Summit glass bell in a clear carnival "Wildflower" pattern. 3.1"dia. x 5.75"h. $30-35.

A. J. Beatty & Sons
1888-1892

United States Glass Company, Factory R
1892-1962

Tiffin Art Glass Corporation
Tiffin, Ohio, 1963-1966

Tiffin Glass Company, Inc.
Tiffin, Ohio, 1966-1979

Tiffin Crystal
Tiffin, Ohio, 1979-1984

Maxwell Crystal, Inc.
Tiffin, Ohio, 1984-1997

Crystal Traditions of Tiffin, Inc.
Tiffin, Ohio, 1997-

Tiffin produced bells from molds from companies that went out of business and decorated them with various engraved and etched patterns. By 1940 the Tiffin label was used on all their glassware. Some bells were signed "Tiffin". In 1964 Tiffin purchased the molds and equipment of the T. G. Hawkes Cut Glass Company in Corning, New York. Some bells have been produced with the Hawkes name.

A Tiffin clear glass bell with red flashed glass shoulder and seven knop handle. 3"dia. x 6.25"h. $30-40.

A Tiffin clear glass bell with an etched "Queen Astrid' pattern and a 7 knop handle. 2.9"dia. x 6"h. $35-45.

A pair of Tiffin clear glass bells with an engraved lovebirds decoration. The cranberry glass bell is signed C. King and is 2.75"dia. x 6"h. $40-45. The clear glass bell is 3"dia. x 6.25"h. $35-40 each.

A pair of Tiffin cut glass bells in a cut 17624 "Eterne" pattern, 2.9"dia. x 5.25"h. on the left and a cut 17679 "Empire" pattern, 2.6"dia. x 5"h. on the right. $40-45 each.

A Tiffin Hawkes cut glass bell. 3.4"dia. x 8.25"h. $40-50.

A pair of Tiffin cut glass bells in a cut 17623 "Seville" pattern, 3"dia. x 6"h. on the left, and a cut "Squire" pattern, 3"dia. x 6"h. on the right. $40-45 each.

A Tiffin clear glass bell in an etched floral pattern, 599 on stem 2823. 3.4"dia. x 7.5"h. $30-40.

A Tiffin green glass bell in a Killarney 17394 pattern. 3.5"dia. x 5.75"h. $35-40.

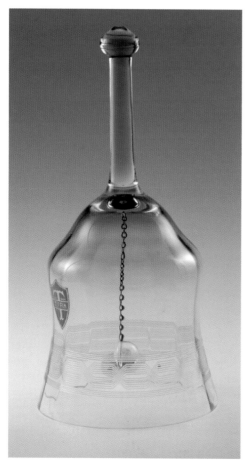

A Tiffin clear pink glass bell with engraved bands. 3.1"dia. x 6.5"h. $30-40.

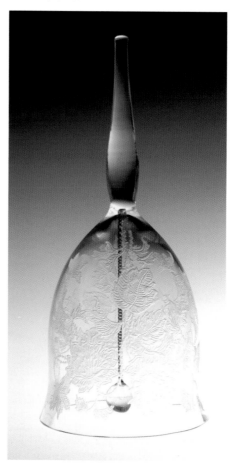

A Tiffin clear glass bell in an etched floral pattern, 599 on stem 2823. 3.4"dia. x 7.5"h. $30-40.

A Tiffin "Punties in Square" cut 17431 pattern. 3.5"dia. x 7.25"h. $40-50.

A Tiffin Clear engraved glass bell with a vaseline handle. 3.4"dia. x 6.6"h. $50-60.

A Tiffin clear glass bell with an etched floral "Renaissance" pattern. 3"dia. x 7.25"h. $30-35.

New Martinsville
Glass Company
1900-1944

Viking Glass Company
1944-1987

Dalzell-Viking Glass Company
New Martinsville, West Virginia, 1987-1998

Blown glass bells are known from the Viking Glass Company and its successor firm, the Dalzell-Viking Company.

A Viking violet cabbage leaf design glass bell. 3.75"dia. x 5.75"h. $25-30.

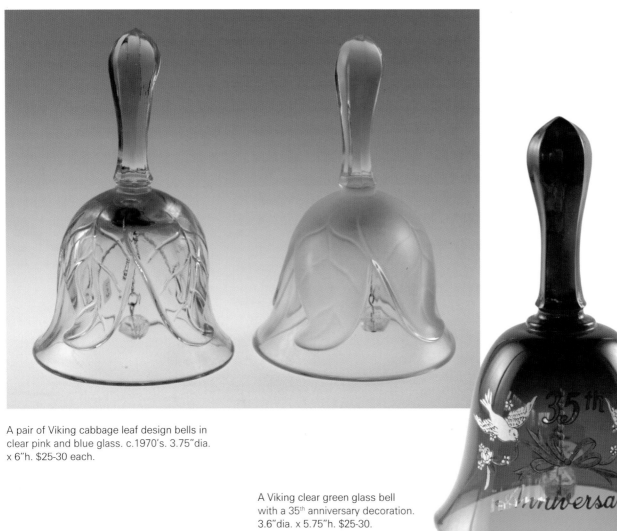

A pair of Viking cabbage leaf design bells in clear pink and blue glass. c.1970's. 3.75"dia. x 6"h. $25-30 each.

A Viking clear green glass bell with a 35th anniversary decoration. 3.6"dia. x 5.75"h. $25-30.

A Dalzell Viking 25th anniversary glass bell. 2.75"dia. x 6"h. $25-30.

A pair of Viking frosted glass bells with painted cardinal on the left and painted flowers on the right. 3.25"dia. x 7.75"h. $20-25 each.

A pair of Viking glass bells in an orange and green "Country Craft" #7921 pattern from 1979. 3.5"dia. x 5.75"h. $30-35 each.

Westmoreland Glass Company
Grapeville, Pennsylvania, 1924-1985

Westmoreland started producing glass bells in 1975. Today they are known primarily for having produced many 6" cameo glass bells as well as smaller 5" bells during the 1970s.

Six Westmoreland cameo glass bells in Line #754. They were produced from 1978 to 1980. Many were decorated with roses, cameos, or Beaded Bouquet inside the oval cameo. 3.5"dia. x 6.5"h. $30-35 each. *Courtesy of Mary and Ken Moyer.*

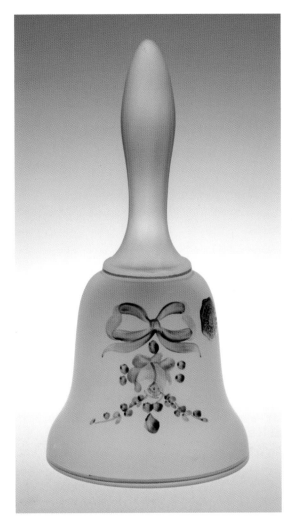

A Happy Anniversary glass bell made in Japan for Westmoreland. 2.25"dia. x 5.1"h. $15-20.

A Westmoreland frosted glass bell with painted roses and bow. 2.5"dia. x 5.1"h. $20-30.

R. Wetzel Glass
Zanesville, Ohio, 1974-1985

Wetzel made some kewpie doll and owl glass bells. Some are signed.

Far right:
A Wetzel blue carnival glass owl bell. 2.4"dia. x 4.9"h. $40-50.

Right:
A Wetzel white carnival glass kewpie doll bell. Signed R. Wetzel on the top inside of the bell. 2.25"dia. x 5.1"h. $35-45.

Wilkerson Glass Company
Moundsville, West Virginia, 1975-

The Wilkerson Glass Company is noted primarily for their production of glass paperweights. However, when the Guernsey Glass company went out of business Wilkerson purchased the mold for the smocking pattern glass bell and has produced several glass bells using that mold. The mold originated with the Akro Agate Glass Company. The top inside of the bells still have "Made in USA" from Akro and "B" for Bennett from Guernsey, but above the Made in USA is a molded "W" for Wilkerson.

A Wilkerson clear smocking glass bell in a vaseline color. 3.25"dia. x 5.75"h. $55-65.

A Wilkerson dark blue carnival glass bell in a smocking pattern. 3.4"dia. x 5.6"h. $40-50.

A Wilkerson blue slag smocking glass bell. 3.4"dia. x 5.6"h. $60-70.

L. G. Wright Glass Company
New Martinsville, West Virginia, 1937-1999

L. G. Wright had other glass companies produce bells from original or new molds. Several bells are known in the Daisy & Button pattern and some of these were made, with and without clappers, as covers for candy boxes in the 1960s.

Candy boxes are known in clear colorless glass, blue, green, amber, vaseline, frosted gold, and frosted yellow glass, the latter known with a clapper in the bell cover. Bells with glass clappers are known in red, blue, green, amber, frosted yellow, chocolate, and clear colorless glass.

The bells and candy boxes were made for Wright by Westmoreland and Fenton. Red, blue, green, amber, and vaseline bells were made in the 1950s and 1960s. A chocolate glass bell was made around 1983 by Fenton. The clear colorless glass bell was made in 1990-1991.

Because of identical handles some bells with a Currier & Ives pattern sometimes have been identified as being made by Wright, but they are much older and were made by the Co-operative Flint Glass Co. of Beaver Falls, PA in the late 1880s and early 1890s as bells and covers for butter dishes.

A pair of Wright green glass daisy & button covered candy dishes. 8.75"h. $40-50 each.

A Wright clear colorless daisy & button glass covered candy dish. The bell cover has a clear crystal clapper.

A Wright red daisy & button glass covered candy dish. 8.75"h. $50-60.

A pair of Wright amber glass daisy & button covered candy dishes. 8.75"h. $40-50 each.

A pair of Wright yellow glass daisy & button covered candy dishes. 8.75"h. $40-50 each.

A pair of Wright blue glass daisy & button covered candy dishes. 8.75"h. $40-50 each.

Unknown

There are many bells believed by the author to be products of American companies made of cut glass, pressed glass, blown glass, stained glass, engraved glass, and borosilicate glass. However, at this time the makers are unknown to the author.

A clear cranberry glass bell with cut to clear punties and rings and a clear colorless handle. 1.75"dia. x 2.75"h. $60-75.

A clear glass bell with a cut star pattern and 6 knop handle. 2.25"dia. x 5.1"h. $30-35.

A milk and pink slag glass bell with a molded vertical side pattern and horizontal pattern on the round handle. A beaded chain clapper slides through the top. A similar bell is more commonly seen in clear glass. 2.9"dia. x 3.6"h. $25-30.

A clear glass bell with frosted, blue, and gray striping with a rectangular shape handle. 2.25"dia. x 2.9"h. $30-40.

A clear glass bell with a ruby two part handle and a clear clapper with colored seeds. 2.25"dia. x 4.9"h. $25-35.

An old clear blown glass bell with a cork in the hollow handle holding the clapper. 4.25"dia. x 7"h. $60-70.

An American 19th century clear purple glass bell with a replaced clapper. The pattern is similar to other bells with a flat metal clapper on a stiff wire held to the glass by a cork imbedded in the glass. 3"dia. x 5"h. $50-60.

A clear glass bell with a golden eagle handle. 1.9"dia. x 5"h. $15-20.

A clear glass bell with a thumbprint border and a perfume bottle clapper labeled P. N. Perfume. 3.75"dia. x 6.5"h. $40-50.

A Clear glass bell with hollow handle decorated with white striping. The bronze chain and clapper indicates that it was made no later than the 1920s. 2.5"dia. x 5.5"h. $30-40. *Courtesy of Marilyn Grismere.*

Three glass Liberty Bell containers that were made to be used initially to hold jelly or other similar material. Then the coin slot at the top was to be opened and the container with a metal bottom cover was to be used as a coin bank. The front amber bell has "Pat. Applied For" on the handle. The patent was applied for on June 16, 1885. The other two bells have "Patented Sept. 22, 1885" on the handle. 4"dia. x 4.25"h. each. $45-55 each. The inventor was J. Frederick Loeble.

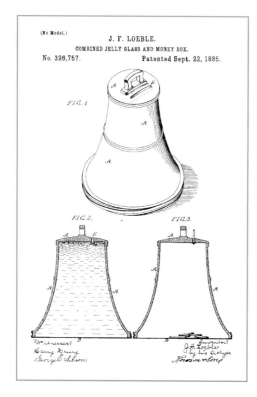

A copy of U. S. Patent 326757 for the Liberty Bell containers.

The metal bottom cover is typical for all the bells. The molded inscription reads "Robinson & Loeble, 723 Wharton St., Phila. PA. Robinson & Loeble was a manufacturer and wholesaler of preserves, mincemeat, and fruit butters during the 1880s.

An amber and clear colorless glass bell with a vintage pattern and hexagonal handle. 3.5"dia. x 7.6"h. $25-30.

A clear multi-faceted blown glass bell with a needle etched scroll along the rim and a clear amber glass handle. 3"dia. x 5.4"h. $50-65.

Four small doll house glass bells made of borosilicate glass. Left to right: a clear glass octagonal shape and flared rim with a clear clapper, 1"dia. x 1.75"h.; a cranberry clear glass with colorless handle, 0.6"dia. x 1.25"h.; a clear colorless glass, 0.6"dia. x 1.1"h.; a pink to clear glass, 0.25"dia. x 0.75"h. $20-25 each.

A stained glass multicolor bell. 2.5"dia. x 6.6"h. $30-40.

A stained glass bell with leaded partitions. 2.5"dia. x 4.5"h. $50-60. *Courtesy of Mary and Ken Moyer.*

Chapter Four

Lampwork Bells

Many companies have made bells of various sizes by heating
and manipulating glass over a small flame.

Robert Carson
Corning Museum of Glass, Corning, New York

Some glass workers at the Corning Museum of Glass occasionally produce a glass bell

A clear glass bell with a blue wing hummingbird
handle made by Robert Carson of the Corning
Museum of Glass. 2.5"dia. x 6.75"h. $30-40.

National Potteries Corporation, NAPCO
Bedford, Ohio, 1938-

The National Potteries Corporation has produced glassware as well as pottery. Some glass bells are known.

Three Napcoware, Japan, clear glass bells. Left to right: clear deer handle, 3.1"dia. x 6.25"h.; etched oak leaves with a red deer handle, 3"dia. x 6.5"h.; and frosted pink unicorn handle, 3"dia. x 6.5"h. $25-30 each.

Prochaska Galleries, Inc.
Valley Center, California, 1981-

The Prochaska Galleries studio was started by a former Disneyland glass artist, Kevin Prochaska. Initial production was crystal cake tops, Christmas tree ornaments, and several glass objects for television and movie studios. The studio then began intricate glass sculptures enhanced with hues of gold, including a variety of glass bells.

Three Prochaska Galleries clear glass bells with ruffled rim. Left to right: gilded unicorn head handle, 2"dia. x 4.5"h.; gilded cat handle, 1.5"dia. x 5.5"h.; and gilded butterfly handle, 1.9"dia. x 4.1"h. $30-35 each.

Shades of Gold
Cameron Park, California, 1990-

The company has produced china and crystal, as well as blown and pressed glassware. Some crystal bells have been produced with golden hues.

A Shades of Gold sculptured gold plated dragon handle on a blown gold plated glass bell. 1.1"dia. x 3.75"h. $30-40.

Titan Art Glass, Inc.
Fayetteville, Arkansas, 1989-

The Titan Art Glass company in the past was known for its birds of recycled glass as paperweights and attachments to other glass. Several clear glass bells with colored birds as part of the handles are known.

Three Titan Art Glass clear glass bells. Left to right: blue bird top of handle, 2.25"dia. x 7.5"h.; yellow bird top of spiral handle , 3"dia. x 8"h.; and red bird on top of spiral handle, 3"dia. x 8"h. $30-35 each.

Vilhanzano
Montana, USA

Patrick Patterson, known as Vilhanzano, is a world renown glass blower who displays and sells his creations on the internet. He uses glass rods from Italy and makes all kinds of glass blown articles with an occasional bell.

A Vilhanzano (Patrick Patterson) hand blown Italian Glass Lampwork Creations "Isabelle Tessier" bell. 1.1"dia. x 3"h. $50-60. *Courtesy of Sally and Rob Roy.*

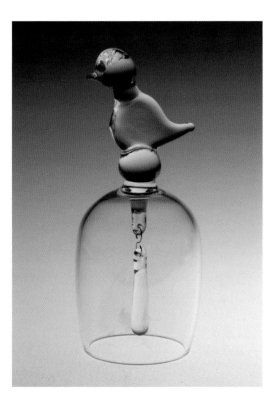

A clear glass bell with a bird handle. 2"dia. x 5"h. c.1971. $25-30.

The maker of some lampwork bells has not been identified.

The American Bell Association

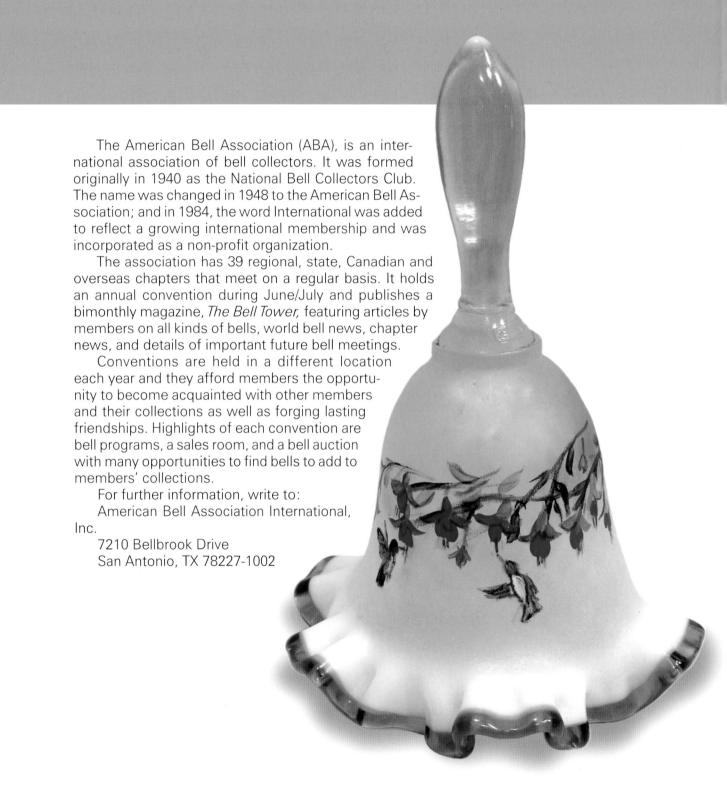

The American Bell Association (ABA), is an international association of bell collectors. It was formed originally in 1940 as the National Bell Collectors Club. The name was changed in 1948 to the American Bell Association; and in 1984, the word International was added to reflect a growing international membership and was incorporated as a non-profit organization.

The association has 39 regional, state, Canadian and overseas chapters that meet on a regular basis. It holds an annual convention during June/July and publishes a bimonthly magazine, *The Bell Tower,* featuring articles by members on all kinds of bells, world bell news, chapter news, and details of important future bell meetings.

Conventions are held in a different location each year and they afford members the opportunity to become acquainted with other members and their collections as well as forging lasting friendships. Highlights of each convention are bell programs, a sales room, and a bell auction with many opportunities to find bells to add to members' collections.

For further information, write to:
American Bell Association International, Inc.
7210 Bellbrook Drive
San Antonio, TX 78227-1002

Index